SIBERIAN SHAMANISM

The **Shanar Ritual** of the **Buryats**

"This glimpse of Buryat culture does not aim to be comprehensive, but it will be fascinating to those interested in Eastern religions and anthropology. Of particular note are the hundreds of full-color photographs that grace the handsomely produced volume; there's also a useful glossary."

PUBLISHERS WEEKLY

". . . fascinating book. . . . With coauthors Zhambalov, a Buryat actor, and Phipps, an African American poet, (Tkacz) gives a vivid and detailed look into this ritual and, more generally, into this rarely discussed culture. . . . This book provides enough information about the culture to place the ritual in context, but it is not meant to be a scholarly treatment of the Buryat culture. The 175 accompanying photographs by fashion photographer Alexander Khantaev are beautiful and convey a sense of color that is not typically associated with this region."

LIBRARY JOURNAL

SIBERIAN SHAMANISM

The **Shanar Ritual** of the **Buryats**

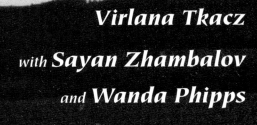

Virlana Tkacz

with **Sayan Zhambalov**

and **Wanda Phipps**

Photographs by
Alexander Khantaev

Inner Traditions
Rochester, Vermont • Toronto, Canada

Inner Traditions
One Park Street
Rochester, Vermont 05767
www.InnerTraditions.com

Text, translations, and photographs copyright © 2002, 2015 by Yara Arts Group

Originally published in 2002 by Parabola Books under the title *Shanar: Dedication Ritual of a Buryat Shaman in Siberia as conducted by Bayir Rinchinov*

Library of Congress Cataloging-in-Publication Data
Tkacz, Virlana, 1952-
  [Shanar]
 Siberian shamanism : the shanar ritual of the Buryats / Virlana Tkacz ; with Sayan Zhambalov and Wanda Phipps ; photographs by Alexander Khantaev.
    pages cm
 Originally published: Shanar. New York : Parabola Books, 2002.
 Summary: "An intimate account of an ancient shamanic ritual of Siberia"— Provided by publisher.
 ISBN 978-1-62055-431-9 (pbk.) — ISBN 978-1-62055-432-6 (e-book)
1. Shamanism—Russia (Federation)—Buriatiia. 2. Buriats—Religion. I. Zhambalov, Sayan, 1966- II. Phipps, Wanda. III. Title.
 BL2370.S5T49 2015
 299'.42—dc23
                                                                    2015019692

Printed and bound in India by Replika Press Pvt. Ltd.

10 9 8 7 6 5 4 3 2 1

Text design and layout by Studio 31, www.studio31.com
This book was typeset in Tiepolo with Zapf Chancery and Sabon as display fonts

Front cover photo: Spirit enters shaman Bayir Rinchinov
Half title page photo: Shaman Bayir Rinchinov instructs Volodya Zhaltsapov
Title page photo: Shaman Bayir Rinchinov

To send correspondence to the author of this book, mail a first-class letter to the author c/o Inner Traditions • Bear & Company, One Park Street, Rochester, VT 05767, and we will forward the communication, or contact the author directly at **www.brama.com/yara**.

Contents

PART I   THE PREPARATION

PART II   CALLING THE SPIRITS

Foreword
to Siberian Shamanism

By Itzhak Beery

This remarkable book follows Volodya through his personal odyssey to be initiated by Spirit, which needs to enter his body. He needs the help of his ancestors' spirits and the support of his community—a powerful metaphor that can touch us all, reminding us of the importance of being in close contact and in harmony with our ancestral and land spirits. Although Volodya's struggle may not seem logical to many in our modern society, it is one we can easily identify with emotionally and symbolically.

Many years ago in my neighborhood in New York City I found myself, entirely by coincidence, glued to my seat with an open mouth, riveted as I watched the *Flight of the White Bird* at La MaMa Experimental Theater Club. Unprepared, I was transmuted through magical layers of realities where time and space ceased to exist. This Yara Arts Group performance was conceived and directed by Virlana and was based on a legend of the Buryats, an indigenous people in south Siberia. It delicately wove spoken words with songs, music, movement, rituals, and ceremonies. It was like nothing I had seen before. I may not remember all the story's details, but I still feel its power in every part my physical and emotional bodies. In that short time I developed a deep emotional identification with the heroine. It was as if we were all transported to the expanses of the steppes, but really it could have been anywhere. It had no specific timeframe but could have been at any time. Although it was a story of one person it had a universal message rooted in the common human experience, connecting the sum of our lives with the Great Mystery of life.

Since then I have attended other productions by her company. Each time Virlana captured the magical dualistic nature of our world—the interaction of the seen and unseen worlds—and brought it into our lives. I believe you will experience this while reading the story Virlana wrote with Sayan Zhambalov and Wanda Phipps and seeing Alexander Khantaev's beautiful authentic pictures of the Shanar—the shaman's dedication ceremony.

You will witness the power of the rituals and ceremonies shamanic traditions have held for millennia all around the world wherever humans exist. We need this understanding to feel wholly connected—with all our senses—to the entirety of the universe around us. In many ways, like the initiate in this book who struggles to gain acceptance from the spirit world, we as a society struggle to be accepted and authenticated as the guardians of the earth.

If you pay attention, you will notice there is a rumbling under the surface of the mainstream controlled media today. It's an undercurrent of hot lava oozing from the depth of people's souls. It carries with it deep passion and old yearnings. It's a burning desire of millions of people around the world—mostly in the technologically advanced societies—to fully re-experience the world with all their sensory capacity as their ancestors did many thousands of years ago. It is a strong desire to be engaged with flesh and blood communities, to experience the magic and mystery of life through rituals and ceremonies.

The statistics on Shaman Portal (www.shamanportal.org), the website I founded as a hub for the global shamanic community, show that more than three quarters of the visitors come from the United States and Europe, and in the United States most are from San Francisco's Silicon Valley and New York City. I believe it is not by coincidence.

Today we are waking up to the realization that our "primitive" ancestors held the secret key to fully understanding and embracing the physical and spiritual world. That knowledge enabled them to live sustainable lives in balance with Mother Earth and themselves. A skill we as a "modern" society have forgotten and run away from. Many in our Western culture are now embarking on a journey of remembrance of who we humans truly are. We are rediscovering the intimate interdependent relationship between the natural world, the spirit world, the entire cosmos, and us. I believe we are too sophisticated, educated, and well informed these days to uncritically conform to governments' rules, corporate media messages, medical and insurance institutions' regulations, and most of all organized religions that dictate how to live our lives, what to believe in, and how to think. We urgently want to independently find that wisdom from the source, the spirit world. We can find this in shamanic practice through ancient ceremonies and rituals, which provide that direct connection to source.

The practice of what we call shamanism is slowly rising to the surface. Movies, books, music, and computer games with shamanic characters and themes are abounding. Thousands of people are going to South America and other continents every year to experience first hand encounters with plant medicine and life changing visions. Thousands are traveling to all the corners of the Earth to participate in workshops and trainings in an effort to reconnect with their spirit guides, reclaim their full potential, and awaken their shut down senses.

I'm convinced that we human beings are truly living in multi-dimensional realities. As humans we have the ability to perceive knowledge, images, and information otherwise hidden from our limited range of senses by shifting from the earthly plane into a shamanic state of higher vibrational consciousness. I'm convinced that this ability has been central to humans' survival from the moment we first walked on this planet.

As the ancient Inca prophecies point out, beginning in 1993 we entered into a new Pachacuti, a five-hundred-year period of realignment and correction of the human journey and consciousness. It is time to be awakened and accept our true nature by living in equilibrium and harmony between the two opposing and complementary forces of the feminine and masculine that exist within each of us. It is a time to take the long overdue journey from our minds to meet our hearts. Only then, when the heart and the mind accept each other in harmony, can we resolve war, poverty, and environmental destruction to ensure future generations' survival.

The big sensory shutdown is real. Look at the millions of eyes that are relentlessly glued to the two-dimensional screens of our smartphones, tablets, computers, and TVs. Aren't we becoming handicapped, dependent, and purely apathetic as we trade in our birthright sensual gifts and abilities for the gifts of technology? The practice of shamanism through rituals, ceremonies, and life stage initiations helps us reestablish a sense of awe of the universe. It helps us gain a new perspective on life and recognize our ability of "seeing" or intuition—our sixth sense.

As you read through this extraordinary account, see the striking pictures, and recite the chants, I am certain you will be transported into that world yourself. You will get to know the human side of the shamans, fall in love with the sacred grounds, learn about the sacred ritual objects, witness the cleansing ceremonies, and participate in the offerings for the sacred land, ancestors, and spirits. You will go through the doubts and tribulations of the initiate and of his community and celebrate his triumph as spirit finally embraces the new shaman. Volodya's personal accomplishments come to ensure the successful continuation and well being of his lineage and that of the whole community into the future. It is a blueprint for modern society to ensure our own fragile future as well.

ITZHAK BEERY is an internationally recognized shamanic healer, teacher, and author. He was initiated into the Circle of Twenty-Four Yachaks by his Quechua teacher in Ecuador and by Amazonian Kanamari Pagè. He has also trained intensively with other elders from South and North America. The founder of ShamanPortal.org and cofounder of the New York Shamanic Circle, he is on the faculty of New York Open Center. His work has been featured in the *New York Times* and on films, TV, and webinars. An accomplished visual artist, owner of an award-winning advertising agency, and author of *The Gift of Shamanism* and *Shamanic Transformations*, he grew up on Kibbutz Beit Alfa in Israel and lives in New York. His website is www .itzhakbeery.com.

Foreword
to Shanar

By Dashinima Dugarov

Shamanism is one of the early forms of religion. An essential trait of shamanism is the belief that certain people, known as shamans, possess the supernatural ability to enter into a state of ecstasy during which they have direct contact with spirits and deities. In this state, the shaman can influence the spirits, discover the reasons for various problems that have appeared in a person's life and correct them through rituals, offerings, and prayers.

The word "shaman" originally is in the Tungus language and means "frenzied" or "possessed." The Russians, who colonized Siberia in the beginning of the seventeenth century, first encountered this phenomenon among the Tungus people and adapted the local word. They then used this word to describe the leaders of all the indigenous ritual cults of Siberia, ignoring local names, such as *oyun* (used by the Yakuts), *boo* (Buryats), *kam* (Turkic-speaking people of Central Asia). In contrast, all Turkic and Mongolian-speaking people called a shamaness *udagan*. This seems to indicate that in Siberia female shamanism is older than male shamanism.

According to a Buryat myth, in ancient times people did not practice any form of religion, worship any deities or make any offerings. This did not please the heavenly beings so they sent to earth one of their own children in the form of an eagle. The first human this eagle encountered was a woman. The eagle gave her the shamanic gift of *udkha*, the hereditary shaman root spirit. The woman who received this gift then became a shamaness, the guardian and priestess of the hearth or *udagan*. The word *udagan* comes from the ancient Turkic word *ot* or *ut* which means fire. From this original female Black shamanism eventually arose male

Black shamanism or *Kharyn shazhan,* which is connected to the Lower World and its fierce ruler Erlyk Khan.

At the same time in the southern forest and grassland regions of Siberia and Mongolia there existed a cult that worshiped the Heavens (*Tengeri*) and Earth-Water (in ancient Turkic *Yer-Sub* or *Gazar-Uhan* in Buryat). This form of ancient Central Asian polytheistic religion is sometimes called *Tengerism,* or White shamanism. Its leaders (the priests of *Tengerism*) are called *boo.*

The contemporary Buryat-Mongolian word *boo* comes from old Mongolian *beki.* When Chinggis Khan (or Genghis Khan, as he is known in the West) came to power, the first person to receive this title was the oldest man in the Khan's Golden Clan. Usun the Elder wore white robes, rode a white horse and was seated above the Khan himself during official court proceedings. How do we explain all this?

Chinggis Khan worshiped the god of the Heavens, *Khukhe Munkhe Tengeri* (The Eternal Blue Heavens), which is not personified. This was the traditional god of Chinggis Khan's Clan and of the majority of the Mongols at the time. Usun the Elder, who was Chinggis Khan's uncle, was the highest priest and as the priest of the god-creator was formally higher in rank than the Khan himself. The word *beki* is not a Mongolian word in its origin. It was most likely borrowed from the ancient Turkic *bag* which meant "god" or "king," which in turn was borrowed from the Indo-European word *bhaga* or "god." The fact that *beki* was not an indigenous word points to the likelihood that Central Asian *Tengerism* was adapted from another culture.

So where did Central Asian *Tengerism* come from? The religious term *tënri,* which means both "heaven" and "god" and the term *tënrici* or "sacred servant of god" were widespread among ancient Turkic people and appear in Orkhono-Yenisei runic tablets from the fifth to eighth centuries. The widespread use of the term *tëngrichi* among the ancient Turkic people attests to the fact that even at that early time (and probably long before that since the term *tengeri* in the form *chengli* was already used by the Huns by the third century B.C.) there existed among the ancient Turkic-Mongolian people a cult of the Heavens, that is, White shamanism with White shamans as its sacred servants and priests.

The earliest worshippers of a god of the Heavens were the

ancient Sumerians. It is our opinion that what is known as White shamanism in Central Asia (that is, the highly developed polytheistic religion of *Tengerism*) was brought by ancient immigrants from southwestern Asia. These immigrants were the cattle-herding Indo-Iranian warriors who arrived in Southern Siberia sometime in the twelfth to eleventh centuries B.C.E. Here they created the remarkable Karasuk culture and a series of related archaeological cultures in the eighth to third centuries B.C.E. Among these were the cultures that produced the slab tombs and "deer stone" carvings of Mongolia and the Baikal area of Siberia. The ancient tribes that created these cultures are the ancestors of the people who now inhabit Central Asia and Siberia, and include the Buryats and the Yakuts. This ancient religion was adopted by indigenous people and continued to function for more than three millennia in this remote part of the Turkic-Mongolian homeland among the Buryats, the Sayano-Altai Turks, and the Yakuts.

One of the splendid rituals of White shamanism among the Khori Buryats—the dedication of a shaman or *Shanar*—is successfully recorded and beautifully described by Virlana Tkacz in this book. I hope that the book finds many interested and receptive readers in America, which is so far away from the Baikal region. I wish it the best on its journey!

FEBRUARY 10, 2002

DASHINIMA DUGAROV is Professor of Ethnography and Folklore at the Academy of Arts of Eastern Siberia, Ulan Ude, Buryat Republic.

My eyes are the shimmering waters
My ears are the echoing forests
My blood is the song of the bison
My dream is the flight of the shaman
My eyes are the drops of the rain
My ears are the howls of the wolf
My blood is pure spring water
My dream is the land of the swan
My brother is the full moon
My sister is the morning sun
My mother is the great earth
My father is the high heaven
My friend is the wild eagle
My blood brother is an unbridled horse
My joy is the blossoming meadow
My sorrow is the ancient song

— Sayan Zhambalov

Introduction

In the summer of 1996 I got off a plane in Siberia and was met by three people whom I had never seen before. They were actors at the Buryat National Theatre, Sayan and Erzhena Zhambalov and Erdeny Zhaltsanov. We were brought together by chance, and struggled to communicate, but soon we realized that we shared the same goals. We wanted to create a new theater inspired and infused by traditional music, song, and legend.

I direct the Yara Arts Group, a resident company at La MaMa Experimental Theater in New York. We bring together fragments of drama, poetry, song, and chant to create original theater pieces. In *Virtual Souls*, the theater piece I had created with my actors, several young New Yorkers surfing the Internet open a webpage and are transported into a Buryat legend. Soon I found myself living our story. I was so enchanted by grandmothers who sang beautiful songs, storytellers who told haunting legends, and shamans who conducted dawn-to-dusk rituals that they became the focus of my life.

The Buryats are an indigenous people who live in eastern Siberia in the area around Lake Baikal. Buryatia became part of the Russian Empire in the seventeenth century when Siberia was colonized. The Buryat-Mongol Republic was created in 1923 as part of the Soviet Union. Today Buryatia is a republic in the Russian Federation and is the home of 300,000 Buryats who form thirty percent of the Republic's population. Buryat language is related to Mongolian, while Buryat religious beliefs are based on Tibetan Buddhism and shamanism.

The Buryats have a rich oral tradition that is still a part of everyday life in the more remote villages of Buryatia. We started traveling to these villages with our Buryat friends, collecting old stories and songs. In the summer of 1997 I brought five Yara

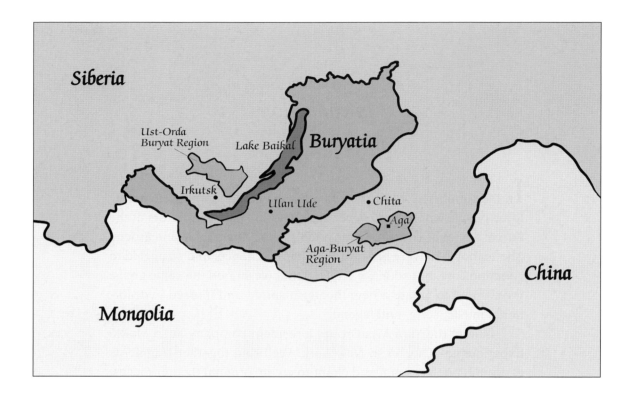

This map reflects the political designations in the summer of 2000. These changed in 2008 when the once autonomous Aga-Buryat Region was merged with Chita and became part of what is now Zabaykalsky Krai, while the Ust-Orda Buryat Region became part of the Irkutsk Oblast.

artists, including poet Wanda Phipps, to Sayan Zhambalov's homeland, the Buryat Aga Region that is located where the borders of Siberia, Mongolia, and China come together. The highlight of our trip was a ceremony that Shaman Bayir Rinchinov conducted for a local family.

I met Shaman Bayir again the next summer when we were performing our new piece, *Flight of the White Bird*, in the cultural centers of the villages where we had originally recorded the material that inspired our piece. Sayan and I came to invite him to attend our performance. Bayir was busy and said that he couldn't come see our show, but added that we shouldn't be too sad because he'd see it in New York. We all laughed, since this seemed beyond improbable.

But sure enough, next March Shaman Bayir attended the opening of *Flight of the White Bird* in New York, thanks to Richard Lanier of the Trust for Mutual Understanding. We were then able to record Bayir's Chant to his Ritual Object. Sayan, Wanda, and I translated the chant and our work was published by *Shaman's*

Drum journal. The following spring, our Buryat friends were in New York again, working with Yara on our new piece. Sayan then told me that Bayir had invited us to come to Aga that summer and record a *Shanar*, or dedication ritual for a shaman.

In August 2000 I flew to Ulan Ude. There I met Sayan and Alexander Khantaev, our photographer. Together we drove seven hundred kilometers to the Buryat Aga Region. We met with Bayir and received his permission to photograph and tape the ritual. This book describes what we saw and heard at that ceremony, as well as on the several other occasions we met with Bayir.

— Virlana Tkacz
January 2002

Authors Virlana Tkacz and Sayan Zhambalov speak with Shaman Bayir Rinchinov

PART I

THE
PREPARATION

My beautiful homeland
Great Mother Earth
Great Father Sky
Listen to me, hear me well.

I started seeing when I was four. . . . Four is very young. I would walk out in nature and I would see things like outlines of people, people who had died, and the local masters of nature. . . . My father had the gift of sight, but my mother did not. My father understood I also had this special gift and he would ask me very specific questions. If I saw someone on a horse, he would ask me: "What kind of rider do you see? What is he wearing? What color is his horse?" They were very concrete questions because he wanted to understand how clear my visions were, how specific. . . . I knew they were spirits not people because they were transparent. I could see the trees behind them. I could see right through them. At first I only saw my blood-relatives. Then I began to see local masters of nature. Then I started seeing traveling spirits, who were moving from one world to the next. . . .

A shaman is chosen by his family tree—through the generations. The ancestors choose who will be the shaman in the clan and send a mark other people recognize. Sometimes people make a mistake and this can be very dangerous. Sometimes a child gets sick and people start thinking it's shaman sickness, but it is only a child being sick. The rituals are there to test and make sure that no mistakes are made because the consequences can be disastrous.

— Bayir Rinchinov

Shaman Bayir Rinchinov

On a good day

At a good time

Mountain trees were pulled out with their roots.

Mountain trees were cut at the root.

Each leaf was made golden.

Each branch was silvered.

The Sacred Grounds

Shaman Bayir Rinchinov told us that the sacred grounds for the ritual would be ready on Sunday, August 19, 2000. The appointed place for the ritual was a large grassy meadow surrounded by gentle rolling hills. There were no shrines or temples. Here in the "lap of Nature," as old Buryats say, everything has a spirit—not only people and animals, but also trees, rivers, and mountains. A shaman mediates between the world of humans and the world of spirits. The spirits of nature help him in this process.

The tree that the Buryats respect and call their "family tree" is the birch. During a ritual the birch is a conduit between people and the world of the spirits. In special places large birches were dug out with their roots, and smaller birch saplings were cut down at the root. They were brought to the ritual grounds with all their branches and leaves intact. Here they were dec-orated and set into the ground in a traditional pattern, as an offering to the spirits.

Two birch groves were set up. At the south end the men dug a large hole for a tall, thin birch. This birch was the *Serge*, or the Hitching Post.

They lined up eighteen small saplings behind it to form the southern birch grove. Just north of them they lined up eighteen birch
saplings to form the northern grove. Two large holes were dug on
the north end for two big birches. One of the birches was the
Mother Tree, the other was the Father Tree. The ritual was to be
a *Shanar*, a dedication ceremony for a shaman. This is a ceremony
of protection for the shaman and an offering the shaman brings
to his ancestor spirits. If these spirits accept his offering and agree
to protect him, he will become a more powerful shaman. The
Mother Tree was dedicated to the shaman's mother's family, the
Father Tree to his father's clan.

The women ripped fabric to decorate the trees. Each tree had
a *hadak* or silk ritual cloth tied to its very top. Sky-blue ritual cloths
fluttered on the birches in the north grove, and white ones decorated the birches in the south grove. Each branch of every tree was
also decorated with small strips of cloth. White and blue strips
were tied together on some of the branches, while yellow and red
ones decorated others. Bayir told us that the yellow and red strips
signified the female and male origin of everything, while the white
and blue strips were Buddhist in origin.

The children practiced two chants for the ritual. They would
sing: *"Ahe-yohe mini go/Ai don baydgo mini go"* with the Black
shaman and *"Padme hum om mani"* with the White shaman.

"The swan is our mother and the birch our family tree," say the old Buryats. The Khori Buryat Chronicles begin with the story of a hunter, Khoridoi Mergen, who discovers nine wild swans shedding their swan dresses to become beautiful girls. He steals one of the swan dresses while the girls are swimming in Lake Baikal. Startled, most of the swans fly off, but one is left behind to plead with the hunter for her swan dress. He refuses to return it, but marries her. Together they have eleven sons, who eventually head the eleven Khori Buryat clans. One day, when the sons are all grown, the Swan Mother begs Khoridoi to let her try on her old swan dress. Khoridoi at first is reluctant; then he shuts the door of the tent and carefully pulls the swan dress from its hiding place. As the wife puts on the dress, she transforms into a swan and flies out of the smoke hole in the center of the tent. To this day the Khori Buryats await the return of their Swan Mother. They sprinkle milk every morning and pray that she'll come back to their land.

The shamans at this ritual were both Black and White. Black and White in this case does not mean good and evil, but rather defines two different traditions of shamanism. A Black shaman beats a drum while chanting and calls on the spirits of the earth. White shamans ring a bell as they chant. Black shamanism is believed to have arisen in the Lake Baikal area. The origins of White shamanism are less clear. Some scholars believe that White shamanism contains fragments of an old Mesopotamian religion, brought to this area thousands of years ago. Others point to the obvious influence of Buddhism.

Black and White were united
For this full white *Shanar*

In the Buryat Aga Region of Siberia, where the borders of Russia, Mongolia, and China come together, Black and White shamans conduct rituals together. The Buryats here are Khori Buryats, descendants of Khoridoi Mergen and the Mother Swan. They consider themselves to be Swan people —descendants of Heaven who can unite the Black and the White.

During this *Shanar* Black and White shamans took turns conducting the various rituals. The White shamans used the southern birch grove, while the Black shamans used the northern grove. Most of the shamans in Bayir's circle practice on both Black and White sides, but each shaman has a preference for one. Bayir, as the leader of the group, would usually choose the Black side, which is considered to be more powerful. The other Black shaman was

Dulma Dashiyeva, a striking woman from Aga. The leader of the White side was the shamaness Seseg Balzhinimayeva.

Bayir, Dulma, and Seseg, now all in their forties, started on the path to shamanism at the same time. Those were difficult times, since shamanism was forbidden under the Soviets. All religions were dubbed "the opiate of the people," but shamanism was considered a particularly odious form that prevented its "unenlightened practitioners" from joining the "progress on the road to socialism." Shamans were portrayed as insane or devilish. The anti-religion campaigns of the 1930s and 1950s were particularly harsh. In the Buryat Aga Region people tell many stories of shamans who defied the authorities, but eventually most were shot or disappeared into the labor camps of northern Siberia.

ABOVE: *Black shaman chanting with drum and White shaman chanting with bell*

BELOW: *Shamans Bayir, Dulma, and Seseg*

On my father's side there were twelve generations of shamans. . . . The last shaman on my father's side was executed in 1924. My father died in 1982. He was persecuted for twenty-one years. . . .

I had a teacher, a woman who did six offering rituals for me, and my father was always there. But my father could not do these types of rituals. My teacher, she conducted the rituals, but it was during the Soviet era. She did not have the power. She would call down spirits, but she could not do more complicated things. She would call down the spirits of her ancestor shamans, but she did not know how to have them inhabit her. . . . Every five years or so another ritual had to be done. The offering was to the ancestors so that for five years my visions wouldn't overwhelm me. But by the fourth year I would start having the visions again and by the fifth year something had to be done about it again. My first teacher died when she was still young. My second teacher was from Mongolia.

— Bayir Rinchinov

OPPOSITE: *Shamans Bato-Bolot, Tuyana, Bolod-Akhe, Olya, and Volodya, the dedicating shaman*

Some shamans joined the exodus of Aga Buryats to Mongolia. Although Mongolia was a Soviet satellite state, the remote Buryat villages of Eastern Mongolia were far from government scrutiny. There the shamans were able to quietly continue their practices. With the easing of Soviet control Aga Buryats started to travel to these villages. Bayir, Seseg, and Dulma, who were then young shamans in search of a traditional mentor, were able to find an old shaman in a Buryat village in Mongolia who became their teacher. And so the ancient traditions, which had been in danger of being lost because of the seventy-year ban, were revived.

In the summer of 2000 times were good because people could openly display their belief in shamanism, but they were also very hard times economically. Seseg once taught kindergarten in her native village, but the government stopped paying teachers in remote villages. Seseg had to think about her family's survival. She decided to get a cow because, as she said, at least the children would always have milk on their lips. So Seseg, educated to be a teacher, now keeps a cow for a living and practices shamanism. Many other educated Buryat villagers were also forced by circumstances to return to their ancient traditional ways.

In addition to Bayir, Dulma, and Seseg, there were several other shamans at the *Shanar* who were only starting on the path to shamanism. They served as assistants to the shamans during the ritual. There was Bato-Bolot, a middle-aged man who preferred to shamanize on the White side, and Tuyana, a young shamaness who preferred the Black side. Then there was the kindly elder Bolod-Akhe[1] from the collective farms far to the south near the great lakes that border on Mongolia, and the beautiful Olya from Alkhanay who had only recently discovered her calling.

The calling to become a shaman usually first appears as a very serious illness that seems incurable. It is known as shaman sickness. The person must acknowledge that the source of the illness is spiritual. They also must accept the fact that they will become a shaman and undergo a ritual before the illness disappears.

The dedicating shaman at the *Shanar* was Volodya Zhaltsapov. He was the reason we were all there. He was the one who was bringing this *Shanar* to his ancestors.

This is the land where he was born,
His homeland.
This tall, pale young man,
Son of Zhalsab,
Is now forty-seven years old
And was born in the Year of the Horse.
Listen to me, hear me well.
He is of the Modon Khargana clan
And is of Buryat bone.[2]

[1] *Akhe* is how Buryats address respected male elders. *Abgey* is the term used for respected female elders.
[2] Traditionally Buryats say they are of Buryat bone, not of Buryat blood. They consider the bone to be their heritage from their father's line. The blood is considered to be the heritage from their mother's line.

OLYA: *Of course, shaman sickness is frightening. The most frightening is the feeling that you don't exist. It's as if someone else is living inside of you. After the sickness, you don't remember anything that happened. It's as if everything was erased. . . .*

VIRLANA: *Did you know right away what it was?*

OLYA: *The first time it happened was after I finished the tenth grade. I was very sick. The second time I got sick they sent me to see a woman in Aga, but I didn't get better. Then I went to the* datsan, *the Buddhist temple. They talked to me and sent me here to Bayir. I came here on the twenty-fifth and on the twenty-seventh they did a Lighting of the Lamp Ritual for me. After the ritual I could sleep at least two or three hours a day. Before that I couldn't sleep at all.*

VIRLANA: *Were you interested in shamanism before?*

OLYA: *(laughs) No, not really. But now I'm learning.*

VIRLANA: *How old are you?*

OLYA: *I'm twenty-four. I was born in 1976.*

In Aga a male shaman is called *boo* and a shamaness *udagan*. The word "shaman" was popularized in the West at the end of the nineteenth century by the Oxford scholar M.A. Czaplicka. It is based on a word used by the Tungus, another indigenous people who live in Siberia. Other people in Siberia call a male shaman *kam*, *oyun*, or *boo*, but all call a female shaman an *udagan*.

Shamanism is an oral tradition in Aga. There is no sacred book that is read and interpreted through generations. Rather, every shaman personally passes his form of shamanism to his students. Shamans learn the chants from their teachers, and then they chant as the spirit moves them. For instance, Bayir told me Tuyana was a very exact person and would say exactly the same words every time she chanted. On the other hand, Dulma was an inspired shaman and rarely said the same things twice.

The history and beliefs of shamanism are also conveyed verbally. During the breaks in the rituals the shamans would tell legends and stories about shamans in the past. These stories were often entertaining and tended to end with a joke. But as everyone laughed important lessons and history were being passed on to the next generation. Most of the stories in this book were told during meals or breaks in the ritual.

The first shaman was an eagle. The spirits made the eagle a shaman to protect the Buryats from evil spirits and acquaint them with the good ones. . . . The eagle descended to earth, but the Buryats could not understand him. They took him for a regular bird and were unaware of his mission. The eagle could not make himself understood, because the spirits had not given him the gift of human speech. Although he could see everything and under-stood why the Buryats were suffering, he could not help them, nor could he protect them from the evil spirits. So the eagle returned to the heavens and explained that he couldn't be a shaman because he couldn't speak. He asked that either he be given the gift of speech or that one of the Buryats be made a shaman.

The spirits thought it was inappropriate for a bird to speak like a human, so they decided to allow the eagle to pass his shaman abilities to the first human he saw. The eagle descended to earth and perched on a tree. A Tungus woman, who had run away from her husband, was sleeping under this tree. The eagle passed his shaman abilities to her and flew back to the heavens. When the woman awoke, she saw everything, she saw the good and evil spir-its, and started to shamanize. She returned to her husband and became pregnant. Some people say she was pregnant with the eagle's child. . . . The boy, who was born to the Tungus woman who received the gift of shamanism from the eagle, grew up and also became a great shaman.

— Shaman legend

Our golden yellow *Shanar*
Is complete.
It unites the Black and the White.
It takes place here beautifully.
It has a Father and a Mother.
It has nine beautiful Children of Heaven.
It has two beautiful Guardians of the Ritual.
It has two beautiful Cupbearers.
Listen to me, hear me well.
Take care of us from both sides.
Help us all together.
Listen to me, hear me well.

The shamans were not the only active participants at the *Shanar*. Our *Shanar* had a ritual Mother and Father and Nine Children. "The Father and Mother are the masters. They are the most important people here and must always lead the Children," Bayir said. The *Yuhengud*, or the Nine Children of Heaven, he said, were there to help the *Shanar's* shaman "get lost," that is, enter into the state of running ecstasy that would propel him up either the Mother or Father Tree. There is a beautiful old shaman text from this area that describes the children as dancing the *Neryelge*, or Thunder Dance.

We play on the rays of the sun
We ride on the rays of the moon

We rise into the heavens
We descend onto the hills

Eight young ones jumped up
They met a loving mother
Nine young ones danced
They met a glowing mother
Three times in the ritual
We will dance the ancient dance
All nine will dance together!
All eight will jump together!

Other important participants included the two Guardians of the Ritual. These young men were responsible for the fire and the sacred smoke. The White shamans burn incense like Buddhists, while the Black burn *Aya-ganga,* a grass similar to the sage that the Native Americans burn at their rituals. There were also two young women called the Cupbearers. They brought milk, tea, and vodka for the ritual. Although vodka was used as part of the ritual, most of it was sprinkled into the air as an offering. Bayir did not tolerate drunkenness at the ritual.

Eastern Buryats make offerings by sprinkling milk or vodka into the air. They dip the ring finger of their right hand into the liquid and then flick it in the Four Directions. Some people also flick towards the Sky and the Earth, while others end by lifting their finger and touching their own foreheads. On special occasions a little birch twig can be used to sprinkle the milk or vodka.

The two Cupbearers Rodna and Aryuna

The nomads of Mongolia and Buryatia have used gers, or round tents, for thousands of years. Gers are made of a wooden frame and covered with felt. The round wall of the tent is made of wooden lattice sections that are tied together with leather strips. The cone-like roof is formed when a round wooden ring with many long spokes is raised. The spokes are spread out to rest on top of the lattice wall and lashed. The form of the ger is very steady and can survive the brutal winds of the Central Asian steppes. The wooden framework is covered with felt, a beaten wool fabric as thick as a carpet. The felt provides great insulation, so it is surprisingly cozy inside a ger, both in the cold of winter and the heat of the summer. Canvas is added on the outside to make the tent waterproof and a wooden floor is placed to protect the inhabitants from the damp of the earth. Traditionally, a fire was set up in the center of the tent and the smoke was allowed to rise up through the smoke hole on top. Today a wood-burning stove is placed in the center of the tent and a metal stovepipe is allowed to stick out the smoke hole.

The only structure on the sacred grounds was a large round tent called a *ger*. Traditionally, a *ger* is always set up so that the door faces south. The northern end of the tent is the sacred area where the host and the honored guests sit. During the *Shanar* an altar was set up in the northern end. The Black shamans chanted to the west of the altar, while the White shamans chanted to the east. Usually, men sit in the west portion of the tent, while women use the east end. But during the *Shanar* the Nine Children of Heaven occupied the western part, while the Mother and Father of the ritual, as well as the rest of the participants, sat in the eastern section.

Three altars were set up against the north wall of the *ger*, with another altar in front. Offerings stood in rows on each table. There were tiny cups of tea, vodka, and milk, as well as a cup with an oil lamp. A glass bottle with the bottom cut off protected the flame. The liquid offerings alternated with cups that held a traditional dry cheese topped with a stack of cookies held together with butter. Sugar cubes and candies decorated each stack. A new shirt was

ABOVE: *The three altars with close-ups below*

String that marked the boundary of the sacred grounds

OPPOSITE PAGE:
Volodya's relative in front of the dining tent

Authors Sayan Zhambalov and Virlana Tkacz

Photographer Alexander Khantaev

Professor Margarita Gomboyeva

placed on the central altar. The eastern table held a dish with incense that the leader of the White side would burn. Seseg traced what looked like the letter "G" in the incense.

As the preparations neared completion, stakes were driven to mark off the sacred grounds. The stakes were tied together with string. There was one point of entry into the grounds. Only the participants in the ritual were allowed to enter during the entire ceremony. Bayir also permitted four people to document the ritual. Three of the people were from Yara Arts Group. Sayan Zhambalov recorded the chants on a digital audiotape, while I videotaped the ceremony. Alexander Khantaev took the photographs that are in this book. The fourth person was Professor Margarita Gomboyeva, from the University of Chita, who specializes in shamanism.

Volodya and his family were the hosts of the event. They had organized all the participants and now had to take care of them during the ritual. Just outside the sacred grounds Volodya's relatives set up an outdoor kitchen. There, over an open fire, they would cook every meal during the ritual.

Many other people who needed healing gathered to see the shaman. Bayir wasn't opposed to Western medicine, and usually would only see people who had been abandoned by medical doctors. He told a pesky petitioner with a toothache to stop wasting his time and go see a dentist. Bayir invited all the people who had come to see him to take part in the cleansing rituals, but then he asked them to leave afterwards. He wanted to focus on the *Shanar* and said he would not have the energy to deal with the other requests. He only allowed three people to stay and said he would see them during the lulls in the ceremony. They were a young boy who screamed at the sun, a girl who had epileptic fits, and a woman with a large swelling on her neck.

But first Bayir had to take care of one of the people in his own circle. Tuyana, the young Black shamaness, had a bandaged hand. Bayir had her unwind the dirty bandage. There was a huge gash in her palm. It was several weeks old. Tuyana had cut her hand on a piece of glass while doing renovations on her apartment. The wound was now infected, but Tuyana was more concerned that

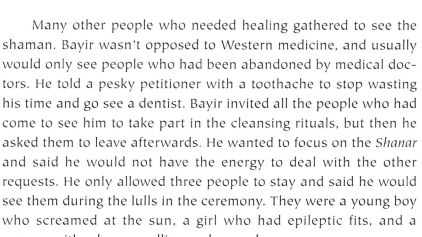

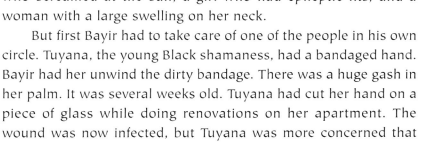

Tuyana holds the power flags in her bandaged hand

she could no longer make a fist. How would she hold her drum? How could she, a Black shamaness, not take part in this ceremony because of a cut? Bayir touched her palm and said he felt a lump at the center of the wound. He rubbed and massaged her hand. He was concerned because she didn't seem to have any feeling in her fingers. As Bayir pricked her fingers with a needle, Tuyana sat calmly unconcerned. Then suddenly she jumped and pulled her hand away. "Well, at least that finger has some feeling," Bayir cheered her up. "Now move each finger one by one," he told her. "And keep moving your fingers, so they don't freeze up." Then he told Bato-Bolot to open up a bottle of vodka. Bayir held Tuyana's hand as he poured the alcohol on the wound. She hissed as the vodka burned and disinfected the wound.

Bayir then told her to go outside to look for a particular plant and put the leaf on the wound before wrapping it up again. I followed Tuyana out the door and told her I had some penicillin ointment if she wanted it. I said I didn't want to interfere with Bayir's treatment and perhaps she should check with him before she decided. She thanked me and said she'd let me know.

Then all the shamans gathered in the *ger*. They tossed a coin to determine who would do which ritual. Bayir lost the majority of the tosses and it seemed he would have to perform most of the rituals on the Black side. But he bargained with Dulma and she agreed to do the chants on the Black side in the beginning.

All the other participants of the ritual were invited into the *ger*. Bayir talked to the children. As the Children of Heaven, he said, they must always be together, holding hands. They must sleep and eat together, and always remain in the same order. "Don't let go of each other, don't let anyone pass between you. Smile. This must all be done with joy.

"We will start now. If all goes well we will finish the day after tomorrow in the morning," Bayir said. Then he introduced the four people who were documenting the ritual. Turning to all the participants, he said, "If you want to eat, let us know. If you want to rest, let us know. We must all walk as one."

The beautiful instrument that I hold
Was crafted, made by
The heavenly white smith. [1]

The Ritual Objects

First, the spirits of the ritual objects had to be called down. They must descend and empower the shaman's instruments before the ceremony can proceed. Some of the ritual objects a Black and a White shaman use are the same, like the headdress. Others serve similar functions, but are essentially different objects, such as the drum and the bell. The chants of the Black and White shamans to their ritual objects differ because of this.

BAYIR'S CHANT TO RITUAL OBJECTS
THE BLACK CHANT

The Drum

From far away, from the
  Northwest
From a distant beautiful
  place
The sound of my drum
Covers the land like a mist.
The beautiful instrument
  that I hold
Was crafted, made by
The heavenly white smith.
I call to you, oh seventy-
  seven smiths.

I bring you strong wine.
I beg you, taste it.
Listen to me, hear me well.
Drink the strong wine [2]
Brought to you by this
  humble son.
Look kindly upon it.
Look after me and protect
  me.
Listen to me, hear me well.

---

[1] Shaman drums are often made by silversmiths or "white smiths," as the Buryats call them.

[2] What is offered is *dezhe*, the dark layer on top of fermented mare's milk that is considered to be the best part. This wine-like drink is often used in Buryat rituals.

SESEG'S CHANT TO RITUAL OBJECTS
THE WHITE CHANT

The Bell

Master of
My blazing white Bell is
The quick chanting translator
For the great family tree of the gods in heaven.
Listen to me, hear me well.
I offer you strong dark wine.
Praying
I offer it to you.
Listen to me, hear me well.

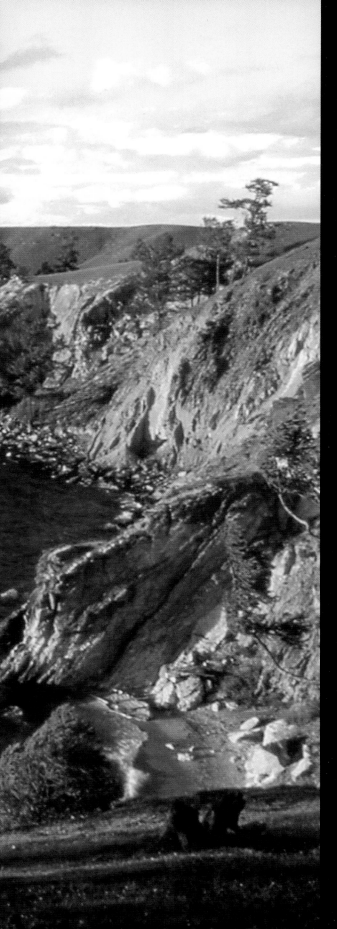

SHAMAN CHANT REFRAINS

The Black and White shamans use different refrains in their chants. Neither of the refrains is in Buryat.

THE BLACK CHANT

**Ahe-yohe mini go
Ai don baydgo mini go.**

Black shamanism is believed to have originated near Lake Baikal where the most sacred place is Shaman's Rock. But the refrain of the Black shaman chant is in a language that people here don't understand. Bayir told us that it refers to Nayan Nova, the utopian homeland of the Buryats believed to be in the foothills of the Himalayas in northern Tibet.

Dashinima Dugarov, who writes on Buryat shamanism, believes that the refrain means "Oh, my Lord Aya, / Let waters from heaven bless this life of mine." It has come down from the ancient Mesopotamian religion. Aya was the God-Creator and the Lord of Thunder in the religion of the ancient Buryats. People prayed to him for rain. The Earth must be blessed with water to be fertile. Raindrops were viewed as seeds from heaven. Even today when it thunders and rains the Buryats say it is a good sign because "Father Sky makes love to Mother Earth."

Shaman's Rock, which juts out into Lake Baikal

THE WHITE CHANT

Om mani padme hum.

This is a phrase in Sanskrit, the sacred language of Buddhism. In Tibetan Buddhism this chant is read as the mantra of compassion for all living beings. In Buryat tradition *Om* refers to the spirits in heaven, *ma* to the local spirits between heaven and earth, *ni* are humans, *padme* animals, and *hum* living things in the waters and under the earth. At ritual the refrain is often sung as: *Padme hum om mani.*

A Buddhist stupa, or reliquary shrine, can be seen through the opening of the Temple Gate arch at the top of Alkhanay Mountain in the Aga Region. This mountain is considered sacred by both shamans and Buddhists. The Dalai Lama visited this site.

TOLI, OR SHAMAN'S MIRROR

Both Black and White shamans wear large metal discs as medallions on their chests. They are called *toli*, or shaman's mirrors, and protect the shaman from evil by reflecting it back.

THE BLACK CHANT

My shaman's mirror is ruled by
The glorious master of the North,
Who is one of the noble born,
Ruler of the great sea,
Father King-Bird.
Listen to me, hear me well.
Your humble son
Calls you with his drum
To his oil lamp with a hundred
    ornaments,
To his altar with six astrological
    signs,
To his beautiful family.
He has faith and invites you with
    open arms.
He is your humble son.
Make eight turns around the
    circle,
Tie your belt and thunder dance.
Listen to me, hear me well.
I offer you strong dark wine.
Accept it with joy.
Taste it with pleasure.
Listen to me, hear me well.

THE WHITE CHANT

Oh, beautiful master of
My silver-white shaman's mirror,
White-haired elder of
My great family tree
Listen to me, hear me well.
Circle round and protect me.
Taste my humble offering.
The offering we sprinkle is as white
    as the sea.
Taste the cream we offer.
Listen to me, hear me well.

BAYIR: Of the Thirteen Spirits of the Baikal, one of the spirits is in the *toli,* the shaman's mirror. He is the master of the mirror. Another is in the drum. Still another is in the *toibur,* drum stick.

SESEG: In Chandali they say there is a place called Tolitin. When we were little, Yunden-Akhe, who is now ninety years old, told us this story. "From the top of the Tolitin Mountain," he said, "we would throw a huge *toli.* It would roll down from the top of the mountain to the river. Then it would circle around and around, turn into a multi-colored lamb and lie down. We would run down to the place where the *toli* fell, but it would no longer be there. We would run back up the mountain and the *toli* was in the same place we found it. Then right before World War II the *toli* disappeared. Then the Russians came. They turned the top of the mountain inside out looking for ore. We thought that our *toli* was gone forever, but in the 1990s it reappeared on the mountaintop. I wonder why it disappeared. Why did that happen?

BAYIR: Probably so that the Russians would not melt it down. That's why it hid itself.

SESEG: When I first had shaman sickness it seemed like two men were always arguing in my head. One would say, "It's like this." The other would say, "No, it's like that." One day my husband told me that the *toli* had appeared again on Tolintin. I climbed the mountain. I found an old *toli*. It was green with age. I placed it against my forehead and said, "Help me." That's how stupid I was then. (All the shamans laughed. They had all been through the pain and confusion of shaman sickness. They also all knew how naïve and hopeless were Seseg's attempts to cure herself. Only a ritual can help someone with shaman sickness.)

BAYIR: When I was just starting, I would dream about a *toli*. Babey[3] would come to me in my dream. In one hand he held a large *toli*, and in the other he held a small one. He would laugh and disappear. I kept on having this dream till it was too much for me to bear. I went to my teacher. It was a cold morning. A little snow had just fallen. He looked at the vodka bottle I brought[4] and said, "Near the sacred place in the Shandan Valley two *tolis* have fallen. Let's go find them." I gathered a few of my friends, Choboloy and a few other young men, and we drove to this area. We got out of the car and my teacher said, "Stop, don't move." It had just snowed and there were no footprints in the snow. He made an offering of wheat grains to the spirits and said, "Outline this area with a silver knife." So I outlined a square three steps by three with a silver knife. "Sit around this," he said and we did so. "Look for it," he said and went back to the car. We started looking, digging. Choboloy dug up the *toli* from under the snow. He found the large *toli*. Then we looked in the area for another half day, but couldn't find anything. My teacher then drank some *arkhe*, or home-brew, and said, "Bayir, give me three coins." He took them and did something with them as he prayed. Then he said, "It is seventy-seven steps from here.

[3] *Babey* is a respectful term for father. It is unclear if Bayir here means his own father, his teacher, or one of the spirits he respects.
[4] One of the ways a shaman can learn about an event is by looking into an unopened vodka bottle that the petitioner brings.

He told me to mark off seventy-seven steps in the southwestern
direction. I started counting off the steps: "One, two, three. . . ."
Just over a small hill was my seventy-seventh step. I stopped and
yelled, "Here is the seventy-seventh step." My teacher said, "Step
aside." He took the three coins and tossed them straight up. The
coins fell in three different directions. He asked me where did the
center coin fall and said, "Go and look for it," I went straight to
the spot and found a *toli* under the snow. To this day these are the
two *toli* on my altar.

THE SHAMAN'S DRUM

Shaman drums drying in the sun on top of a ger, *and inside a* ger *over a fire*

Shaman drums are made of goatskin, which is sensitive to humidity. Before a shaman can use a drum it must be dried over a fire or in the sun. Otherwise, the drum will have a dull sound. During the chant, the shaman holds the drum in front of his face and the sound resonates through his body. The drumming feels like a heartbeat, and the shaman speeds it up and slows it down during the chant.

> The master of this drum
> Whose sound covers this land like a mist
> Is the ruler of the great sea
> The Black Master — Dalzhar.
> Listen to me, hear me well.
> The eight forefathers of Aga
> Of this beautiful grassland,
> Of this beautiful universe,
> I will awaken with the sound of the drum.

The shaman beats his drum with a carved wooden drumstick that has small metal circles attached to it. These jingle every time he hits the drum, as do the small bells attached to the back of the drum.

TOIBUR, OR SHAMAN'S DRUM STICK

My shaman's drum stick
Is ruled by Tolgo — the Heavenly Master
With seventy-seven tongues.
Listen to me, hear me well.
Hard times are here
For your humble children.
Here is something to lean on,
To drum with — the shaman's drum stick.
Then they can get up on their feet and stand.
Tolgo — the Heavenly Master,
Unleash your seventy-seven tongues
And descend.
I offer you strong dark wine.
Accept it with joy.

DULMA: My drum sometimes says: "Not done. Not done." And then at other times it will say: "Done. Done. Done."

BAYIR: Or sometimes it says: "So-so. So-so. So-so. Re-do. Re-do."

SESEG: Recently, I was sitting to the side and I heard your drum say: "Seven. Eight. Seven. Eight." Then I heard it say: "Was heard. Was heard."

SAYAN: Dulma-Abgey, your drum has a male voice.

DULMA: Really, I always think it has a high-pitched voice.

SESEG: No, your drum has a very low voice.

DULMA: Sometimes, when I'm sitting at home, suddenly I see Seseg-Abgey chanting. I clearly see how she sits, how she holds her drum. I can even hear her drum. And then I think, "Oh, Seseg-Abgey has started chanting today." I don't know where it comes from, but suddenly I'm in this state and I can see everything very clearly.

Toibur, or shaman's drum stick, resting on the back of a shaman's drum

MAYKHABSHA, OR SHAMAN'S HEADDRESS

Both Black and White shamans wear a *maykhabsha*, a cloth head-dress with a fringe that covers the face. The headdress also has three long sashes in back. The sashes are made of multicolored pieces of brocade. Each sash ends with a tassel that has a small bell underneath. The only difference between the headdress of a White shaman and a Black one is that the cap of the headdress for a White shaman is made of blue fabric, while the Black shaman's cap is made of black fabric. Both have two large eyes of cloth sewn on the forehead.

THE BLACK CHANT

I put on my beautiful headdress
        with ribbons
And a beautiful red tassel.
It has three beautiful sashes
With a rainbow of colors.
I put on my beautiful headdress
        with ribbons.
The masters who look after me
The guardians of this life of mine
Are the ancestors of my clan
From the beautiful high Argali
Anchored by white rocks,
And supported by Khumgohhan
        Rock.

THE WHITE CHANT

My upper body is protected by
My beautiful headdress with tassels.
Listen to me, hear me well.
Oh, great family tree of gods in
        heaven
Descend as the master
And taste my offering.

BAYIR: The fringe is part of the headdress. It is there to protect the other people in the room. I am forty, but when a very old spirit enters me my face changes drastically. When I am being inhabited I change from the inside out — from the bone out. I change totally. Other parts of the headdress are symbolic like the two eyes and the three long sashes. . . .

Bardag, or Shaman's Whip

Both Black and White shamans have what is called a *bardag* or shaman's whip. The shaman's whip is short and stiff, like a riding crop. The shamans tie it to their hands before they start to chant. When the spirits descend, they often use the *bardag* to bless people. They tap the supplicants on the back with the *bardag* as they call down the blessing. The shamans also use the *bardag* in the cleansing ceremony.

THE BLACK CHANT

The beautiful shaman's whip
    in my hand
Is the master who looks after
    me.
Good-natured shaman's whip
Made from eel skin
And the antlers of a three-
    year-old elk.
The antlers have three
    branches.
Good-natured shaman's whip,
The master who looks after
    me,
The guardian of this life of
    mine.

THE WHITE CHANT

*My red shaman's whip is as
    mighty as an elephant
As it commands and thunders.
The great family tree of gods in
    heaven
Taste my offering.
Listen to me, hear me well.*

Drawing of a bardag. *First cluster from left includes blacksmith instruments: 1) bell, 2) sign of the Four Directions, 3) hammer, 4) hole punch form, 5) shackles for a horse, 6) hole punch, 7) anvil, and 8) tongs. Second cluster includes means of escape: rope, boat with oars, and a ladder. The third cluster includes weapons: 1) bell, 2) fish skin, 3) sword, 4) pike, 5) spears. Parts of the* bardag *identified below it, left to right: a hadak tied to the end, handle made of the horn of a three-year-old stag, center rod of red bush stalks and metal.*

BAYIR: The handle of my shaman's whip is made of the horn of a three-year-old stag. The center rod is made of metal but is covered with stalks from the red bush. There are three clusters of metal ornaments. The bottom one has blacksmith's tools; the middle one has various means of escape, such as a boat with oars; the top one has weapons. Each bundle also has bells.

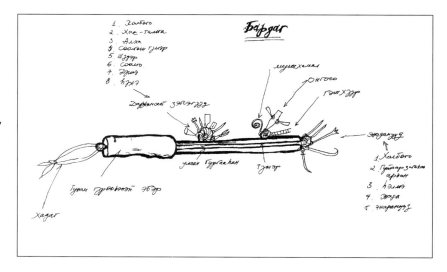

Orgay, or Shaman's Horns

The *orgay,* or shaman's horns, are the most striking part of the Black shaman's outfit. The shaman puts them on when he calls down the spirits.

> He puts on shaman's horns made of clouds[5]
> And is the master who looks after me.
> From the beautiful high Argali
> From the valley of many springs
> From the shepherd's hut known as Khun Khun
> Whose spirit road crosses the Black Pastureland
> Who plays with yellow leaves
> Who drinks from bubbling springs

[5] *Orgay* are usually made of metal.

Whose horse is tied to a birch grove
Who ascended into the stars of the Big Dipper[6]
Like an eagle who spreads his full-fledged wings,
Like a boar whose tusks are full grown,
Like the head shaman who has undergone all the rituals,
Gray-haired father Shambar,
Listen to me, hear me well.
Turn into a rainbow and come
To my oil lamp with one hundred ornaments
To my altar with six astrological signs.
Your humble son requests it.

BAYIR: The horns are usually made from metal — steel, now. They are not realistic depictions of animal horns. A shaman acquires larger horns at special rituals. I have had three big rituals, so mine have three sections.

A shaman would be dressed in the *orgay* for his funeral. Traditionally, shamans were not buried in the ground, but were left exposed on platforms in the treetops. Today there are many stories about emerging *orgay* in this region.

SESEG: In Chandali one of my classmates found an *orgay*. Tseben Dasha Akhe told me, "One day I'm sitting there and I suddenly see my son coming down the street with a set of shaman horns on his head."

BAYIR: We were returning home from a ritual. There were many people in the car. Suddenly we stopped [and we realized that] our road was being closed by an *orgay*. We could not proceed without first finding the shaman horns. We returned to Chadali and spent the night there. In the morning — it was early spring then — we lined up in two rows and spread out across the foothills searching for it. Dolgorma, my wife, found the *orgay*.

---

[6] The Big Dipper is known as the Seven Old Men in Buryat.

Head Administrator for Village: They say Darema saw something like an *orgay,* on the western side of Red Mountain. You know, on the western bank of the river, past the shepherd's hut in the forest. That's where she saw it.

Bayir: My mother used to say, "Bayir, don't go walking there late at night. Two naked men walk there." Maybe she saw something up there. Maybe she also had the gift of sight.

Barlon Akhe: I don't remember who told me this, but one young man from around here climbed up to the top of Red Mountain. He opened a bottle of vodka and sprinkled one glass to the spirits. Then he felt someone put an *orgay* on his head, give him a glass of vodka and say: "Now, go home." He went home with the *orgay* ringing so beautifully on his head. Every time he moved his head he'd hear, "ring, ring, ring." He walked right past the head of the collective farm. He walked into his home and said: "Look, ma," as he moved his head and all the metal rang and rang. His mother took one look, picked up the broom, and started beating him. "Take it back!" she yelled. Suddenly, he came to and saw himself put the *orgay* in its place. Then he saw Regsel Boo holding a huge knife as he jumped up and down in the mist. He was unconscious for three days. But every time he moved his head he heard such a beautiful ringing sound, "ring, ring, ring."

NEMERGE, OR SHAMAN'S CAPE

White shamans do not wear the *orgay*. However, they have a beautiful cape of many colors made of strips of brocade.

> *Oh, great family tree of gods in heaven*
> *You are the masters of*
> *My sky-blue shaman's cape*
> *Which has twelve outer layers*
> *That protect my back.*
> *Each ends with a tassel.*
> *Each tassel ends with many strands.*
> *Listen to me, hear me well.*
> *Circle round and protect me.*
> *Taste my offering.*
> *Listen to me, hear me well.*

DOLGORMA: There was an old woman in Mongolia who made shaman capes. She knew songs that told her which colors to put next while she made the cape and what words to sing as she sewed those parts. She made capes for Seseg and Bayir. But she died. The new shamans go to a good tailor in Aga, but he doesn't know the songs.

THE SHAMAN'S STAFF

Both White and Black shamans have a shaman's staff. The Black shaman's staff is called a *horbo* and it is made of metal. It has a horse head carved at the top and a set of tiny stirrups towards the bottom. A shaman usually has a pair of these and uses them to support himself when the spirit enters him. The White shaman's staff is called a *bayag*. It is wooden and has a dragon head carved at the top with a tiny bell right underneath the head. When Seseg-Abgey chanted and rang the large bell with her right hand, she also twisted the staff back and forth with her left hand, flicking the small bell below the dragonhead to ring in time with her big bell.

A White shaman chants with a bayag *in hand*

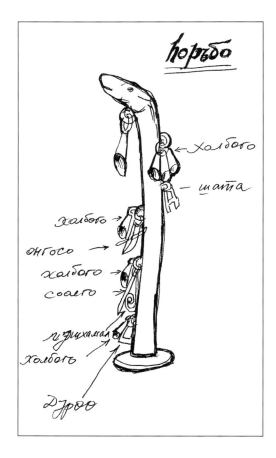

A drawing of the parts of a horbo. *At top right are bells and a ladder that resembles the letter "A." Below left are a bell, boat, bell, awl, rope, bell and stirrup.*

HORBO, OR BLACK SHAMAN'S STAFF

My staff, my beautiful
    shaman's staff
Is the master who looks
    after me.
Heavenly master Khotokhon,
Listen to me, hear me well.
I am your humble son.
The guardian spirit that
    supports me,
My great clan lineage,
Is my beautiful vehicle.
Strong dark wine
I offer three times
To the Heavenly Master
    Khotokhon.
I dedicate the song of my
    drum to you.
Accept it with joy.
Hear it with pleasure.

BAYAG, OR WHITE SHAMAN'S STAFF

Oh, Old White Man,
Come as the master
Of my silver-white shaman
    staff.
Listen to me, hear me well.
I chant and dedicate
Strong dark wine to you.
Taste my offering.
I only offer it to you.
Help me with this ritual.
Accept my offering.
Look after me, protect me
And help me.
Listen to me, hear me well.

TUYANA: On the Black shaman's staff there is a piece of metal that resembles the letter "A" and has a small hole at the center. The number of holes tells you how many *Shanar* rituals this shaman has had. Bayir-Akhe told me that Lubsan Dagba-Akhe, his teacher in Mongolia, could call down his spirit by just shaking the *horbo*.

The Old White Man is a folk figure that appears in both shaman rituals and Buddhist art. He is traditionally portrayed holding a dragon-headed staff. He is considered the guardian of fertility of both people and animals, as well as the Lord of Life and Death.

SHAMAN'S HERITAGE

Both Black and White shamans chant to the ancestors of their family tree.

On Bayir's Heritage
THE BLACK CHANT

Listen to me, hear me well.
My homeland is the Buryat land.
My clan is Batey Khubdud.
My totem animal is the Black Eagle.
Two great shamans
Raised your humble son
At their knee.
I call you with the sound of my drum.
I send you greetings.
I do not speak as a child
But with the strength of thousands.
Accept it with joy.
Hear it with pleasure.
Protect me on my beautiful land
From all Four Directions
Keep an eye on me.
Listen to me, hear me well.

I will awaken with the sound of the drum
The great human family.
I call and invite with open arms.
I will lift from under the black blanket
Bodies transformed by the spirits.
I will call down the Blue Heavens.
Listen to me, hear me well.
I offer you strong dark wine.
Accept it with joy.
Taste it with pleasure.

On Seseg's Heritage
THE WHITE CHANT

May the leader of the White side
Of this beautiful Shanar
Fully complete this ritual
Without mistakes.
The skillful Wagon Master[7]
Of the great family tree of the gods
Is called Seseg.
She is from the Bodongud clan
Whose motto is: "Fly straight into the target."
She calls to you.
Help us.
Assist us from your side.
Circle round and help us.
Listen to me, hear me well.

I will awaken with my soft voice
The sleeping bodies
Of the great family tree
From the far southwest.
Listen to me, hear me well.
I will raise their lying bodies
With the song of my bell.
I will awaken their sleeping spirits
With my precious song
As the leader of the White side
At this golden Shanar.
Circle round and descend
To the song of my bell.
Listen to me, hear me well.

---

[7] The leading shamans at a ritual are called the Wagon Masters.

I ask for

White cleansing waters strong as a storm
For this Golden Shanar.

The Cleansing

After the ritual objects were empowered, the participants of the ritual had to be cleansed. "Have them bring in the iron pot for the cleansing," said Seseg-Abgey. Two men brought in a huge, steaming iron pot. The water it held had just come to a boil on the fire outside. They set the pot at the center of the *ger*. Dulma-Abgey stirred the liquid with a ladle. She raised the ladle and watched the liquid fall back into the pot. In her left hand she held a Buddhist rosary with 108 beads. She counted off a bead each time the liquid fell. Seseg-Abgey started the White Cleansing Chant that at first described the preparations for the cleansing.

> In the beautiful land of Chelutay
> In the valley of Baikal
> At a good time
> On a good day
> From nine points in this valley
> Nine white stones were brought
> According to tradition.
> They were placed in the sacred fire
> Till they were red hot.
> Now having done this, I chant.
> Listen to me, hear me well.
> Come, lead
> Our clan gods and protect us.
> Listen to me, hear me well.
> Water from nine springs
> Was drawn nine times
> According to tradition

And placed over a sacred fire
Till it came to a boil.
Now, having done this, I chant.
Listen to me, hear me well.
Ninety-nine bushes
Were cut at the very root
And brought here
According to tradition.
Now, having done this, I chant.
Listen to me, hear me well.
Om mani padme hum.
The liquid was stirred and poured 108 times.
I ask that our medicine be powerful.
White cleansing waters strong as a storm
Flowing like a spring with my words.

Sing the songs of thunder.
Oh, medicine men with healing hands
Descend here with your songs.
Oh, medicine men with strong prayer beads
Come with powerful medicine.
Listen to me, hear me well.
Come to heal
Our sick.
Conjurers of powerful incantations
Descend and place your strongest words
On my simple tongue.
Send ten thousand incantations.
Our liquid was stirred and poured 108 times.
Give power to our medicine.
Oh, 108 bone-setters[1]
Thunder and sing
For our white cleansing waters strong as a storm
For this Golden *Shanar*.
Give power to our medicine.

---

[1] The bone-setters, or *baryasha*, are folk healers who often also serve as midwives.

After Seseg-Abgey chanted to empower the waters for the cleansing, she prayed for the people who were to be cleansed.

Dulma stirs and pours the liquid 108 times

> They have come together
> From near and far
> To be present.
> Cleanse their bodies.
> Cleanse their spirits.
> Starting at the top
> With the head and the mind.

Then Seseg-Abgey mentioned all the specific parts of the body that should be cleansed because "foul things nest there."

> Cleanse the organs and the bodies
> Of these people
> Without mistake.
> Send down white cleansing waters strong as a storm.
> Thunder as you anoint them with healing waters.
> Listen to me, hear me well.

Seseg-Abgey dipped her *toli* into the healing water.

I stir the silver-white shaman's mirror
In white cleansing waters strong as a storm.
Round and round
I stir them to strengthen our medicine.
Listen to me, hear me well.
Om mani padme hum.
I ring my blazing white bell
And ask
My gods in heaven to
Cleanse these people!

Then, Seseg-Abgey dipped her shaman's bell three times into the cleansing waters.

White cleansing waters strong as a storm
I pray to you and ask
Awaken and thunder
Oh, my gods in heaven
Oh, chanting translator
Oh, medicine man with prayer beads bursting with energy
Oh, medicine man with hands that burst with energy
Oh, conjurers who know powerful incantations
Oh, sorcerers with black curses
Oh, eighty-eight bone-setters
Oh, ninety-nine Wagon Masters
Descend and thunder.
Descend and send down
White cleansing waters strong as a storm.

Seseg-Abgey dipped the bush branches in the cleansing waters and anointed the nine stones three times.

With many prayers
Nine white stones
Were placed in this sacred fire

Heated over this flame red-hot.
Listen to me, hear me well.
Cleanse us with this vapor.
Cleanse us with the smoke
Of yellow-red healing thyme.
Bless and purify
These people
And their bodies.
Cleanse and bless them.
Let them live happily and be blessed.

The two Guardians of the Ritual carried the huge iron pot outside where the White Cleansing Ceremony took place. The shamaness put on a plastic raincoat to protect her traditional brocade robe. The participants of the ritual took off their shirts and lined up. Then one by one they stood in front of the shamaness as she dipped the bush branches into the water. Holding their arms up, they turned clockwise, or "according to the sun" as the Buryats say. As they turned, the shamaness sprayed them with the cleansing water. Older people would hold out those parts that ached and pained them for additional spray. The shamaness also sprayed the water on the nine red-hot rocks. This sent clouds of steam onto the people being cleansed. Afterwards each person was given a piece of paper and told to wipe off the spray, concentrating on the parts that most needed cleansing. The used papers were discarded into one basin.

After all the participants of the ritual were cleansed, all the other people who had come to see Bayir were cleansed. First the men and then the women lined up for the ritual. Afterwards, everyone was told to face north and not look back as the used papers were destroyed. The shamaness chanted for the health of those present and held out her *bardag* or shaman's whip. People bent their heads and one by one walked under her out-stretched arm, accepting the protection of the *bardag*. We were told to brush against the shamaness as we passed under her arm. "But please be careful," Seseg-Abgey said. "Don't knock me over." Finally, each person donated coins and drank the milky cleansing waters out of a large jar.

Dulma-Abgey then chanted on the Black side and did a Black Cleansing. Everyone was invited to take part in the Black Cleansing, which was very similar to the White one. Afterwards the people who had come to see Bayir for healing were asked to leave. As the last of the cars drove out of the valley, the area, which had constantly hummed with human activity and conversations, grew still. Now we started to notice the other sounds present in the grassy meadow and the great blue heavens above.

It was late at night when Dulma started to chant at the small birch sapling and altar placed at the west edge of the ritual site. She then chanted at each birch sapling and altar placed at the Four Directions to seal and protect the sacred area. The participants of the ritual stood behind her, bowing toward the spirits of the direction, then moved on to the next direction according to the sun. Finally, Dulma chanted at the fifth birch sapling and altar placed in the northwest corner of the grounds. It was dedicated to the local masters of nature.

There are many local masters in a given area and they walk a certain path in their domain. People know where these paths are and avoid building on them. The spirits walk these paths at dawn and dusk. A spirit is given a hundred years to protect an area. Often these are the spirits of shamans who did not do enough good in their lifetimes. Now, every good deed the spirit does as a local master gets him one year off, every bad deed gets him one more year.

Dezhyt is the mistress of the area here that includes the sacred grounds. She is in her thirties and is the protector of the birch forest. Some years back the collective farm in this village sent four men to chop down some of the trees in the forest she protects. They got into an argument and shot each other. The police came and took pictures of the bodies. When they developed the film they saw a woman in a traditional costume in the pictures that no one had seen on the scene. It was Dezhyt, the mistress of the forest.

— Bayir

As Dulma-Abgey chanted to seal the grounds, I looked up at the sky and was overwhelmed by the presence of the stars. They shimmered so brightly against the dark of the sky, tempting my hand to fly up and touch them. I had to share this sensation. I turned to the one person who was next to me, since I was last in the line behind the shamaness. It was Professor Margarita. I asked her if she knew which were the stars they say were originally deer that fled into the sky. I had read about it in this wonderful book on Buryat shamanism and I was sure tonight was the night for me to see them. Even in the dark I could see that her look was cold. What good book on shamanism could this American theater director have read? I told her it was the only book I had actually struggled through in Russian. It took me two months, but Dugarov's *Roots of White Shamanism* was definitely worth the effort. "He's my uncle," she whispered. "And he's really something, isn't he?" We nodded together and I felt Professor Margarita's attitude toward me change.

As we retreated to sleep, we were warned not to walk alone at night. Bayir told us that many spirits and animals would be drawn to the area. True enough, at dawn a woman saw a wolf running from the southeast toward the west just beyond the boundary of the sacred grounds. A night guard was set up to make sure no one stole the *Shanar*. A spirit had warned the shamans to watch this *Shanar* without blinking, since someone had an eye on it. All night long we could hear the steady toll of the bell as the Guardians of the Ritual circled the boundary.

An altar to one of the Four Directions

AUGUST 20, 2000

I got up early next morning, grabbed my toothbrush, and headed out to look for a place to wash up. At one end of the grounds I noticed someone with a towel around their neck and headed that way. A little group gathered around a pole that was dug into the ground. On it a clear plastic soda bottle hung upside down at waist height. It was filled with water that trickled out of a hole in the cap once a stopgap was lifted. This ingeniously recycled bottle was our communal faucet.

After I washed up, Tuyana approached me. She told me she had talked to Bayir and he had advised her to use the penicillin. I pulled out my first aid kit. Tuyana unwound her bandage. There was a smell that turned my stomach. I was afraid to look down at her cut. I told her I wasn't a doctor and actually knew very little about medicine. She said she was sure the penicillin ointment would help, but it was very hard to get here. We cleaned her palm with alcohol wipes, spread the ointment on the ragged gash, and tied it up with a clean bandage. I told her we should look at it again the next morning.

We had breakfast in two shifts. First the shamans and the other adult participants ate, then the children. We sat on benches at a large wooden table set up under a tent that served as our dining room. The plates, forks, and cups were labeled with individual names. The Cupbearers placed bowls of food that included boiled meat, potatoes, and a beet salad. They also poured the hot tea with milk that accompanied each meal.

Bayir chants over the cups of milk

Afterwards we all gathered at the northwestern end of the ritual grounds. During a ritual that lasted several hours the Father, Mother, Nine Children, the two Guardians of the Ritual and the two Cupbearers had their souls "knocked out" and sent to the Thirteen Northern Spirits. These spirits are considered the protectors of shamanism and live in thirteen specific places near Lake Baikal. As Bayir chanted, his assistants prepared a cup of milk for each person in turn. The person would say their name and heritage and Bayir would chant for several minutes. Then the cup of milk was placed on Bayir's drum and the person knelt underneath it. Afterwards, they would get up and stand in back of the shaman as he tossed the cup in the northwest direction. If the cup landed

A Child of Heaven kneels under the drum before Bayir tosses her cup

right side up,[2] the person would run to the cup, circle it three times, tear up grass, lift up the cup by holding it with the grass, and drink the remains. Then they had a red tassel pinned to their collar. This was a sign that they were now without their souls.

---

[2] Most of the cups landed right side up that morning. When one cup did land upside down, the shamans read the person's fortune, then chanted and tossed the cup again. This time it landed right side up.

ABOVE: *Bayir prepares to toss the cup of the Father of the Ritual*

OPPOSITE ABOVE: *The Mother of the Ritual kneels to pick up her cup*

OPPOSITE BELOW: *Olya ties a tassel to mark that this Child of Heaven has had his soul sent to the Thirteen Northern Spirits of the Baikal*

"Your souls have left," Bayir said. "Hold on to each other," he reminded the Children. "Don't go anywhere alone." Then he told the Guardian of the Ritual on the Black side to circle them with sacred smoke, but to be extra careful not to touch them. "Don't walk between the Children of Heaven," Bayir told us, "because if you do the youngest one can lose her soul. Once in Chindali when I was doing a ritual for Seseg-Abgey, a woman became so frightened when a spirit descended that she ran between the Children of Heaven and broke their line. The spirit then said, 'If you don't do the *Ekin Khunde* or Clan Ritual by sunrise, the youngest child will die.' The woman who caused all this did not understand what she had done. If this had happened it would have been very bad. Every child here has a mother and father and their own fate.

"We should not be soft with the Children. If they start to nod off, we should make them get up and run. After nine rounds, we should let them rest and then make them get up and run some more. After this experience, they will become stronger. They will understand, if not with their heads then with their legs.

"You see the red tassels on your collar," Bayir told the Children. "At the end of our ritual the dedicating shaman will tie them to his shaman's drum, just like I did." He showed the back of his drum to the Children. "Every time my drum sounds, the spirits of the *Shanar* rise and bring blessings to the Mother, Father, Nine Children of my *Shanar*. Every half year I say a special prayer for the Children who took part in my *Shanar*. After this ritual, when Volodya will beat his shaman's drum, you will be showered with the blessings of the spirits.

"A shaman has no road to the Thirteen Northern Spirits. Even if he were to go right near the Baikal, they will not consider his offering. They will only accept his offering through the Father, Mother, the Children of Heaven, the Guardians and the Cupbearers. . . . If we don't do this part of the ritual, the

OPPOSITE: *Olya holds the red tassels, or* zala

Thirteen Northern Spirits will never accept our offering. I didn't make all this up. Lubsan-Dagba-Akhe told me this. He was an old Buryat who lived in Mongolia. When he told me this I thought he was talking nonsense. But after he died I learned how true what he said was. I started thinking of him as my mentor."

Bayir told the Children that they should take part in this ritual only seven times in their lifetimes. "If a person has their soul knocked out nine times to the Thirteen Northern Spirits," Bayir said, "they become so close to the spirits that they can start feeling like them. They start seeing what is not done well at the ritual. They become bored and start yawning. This is very dangerous for the young shaman." Seseg-Abgey confirmed that this indeed was a danger. Bayir continued, "That is why we never knock out someone's soul more than seven times." Zhamyan, the Guardian of the Ritual on the Black side, said that after he had his soul knocked out he started running the wrong way. "I don't know what is wrong with me," he said, "I feel so lost." Everyone laughed, probably because they knew exactly what he meant.

It is a great offering.
I give breath to it and silver it
With white mother's milk.
I chant and give breath to it.

The Offering

The ritual of knocking out the souls had taken all morning. Now that the participants had been cleansed and their souls prepared, the offerings to the spirits could begin. First, the birch trees had to be brought to life, or "given breath" as Buryats say, so that they themselves could become offerings to the spirits. We walked over to the southernmost end of the birch grove and stood facing the *Serge* or Hitching Post Tree. Just behind this tree there were nine saplings for each of the dedicating shaman's *Shanars*. This was Volodya's second *Shanar*, so there were eighteen of them. At the other end stood the *Zalma* or Offering Tree with its birch altar and offering of traditional white food. Seseg-Abgey, sitting on a small wooden stool, started to ring her bell and chant.

> On the tall white *Serge,*
> At its very white top
> Is a long white silk ritual cloth.
> Every branch is golden.
> Every twig is silver.
> Every bough is decorated.
> The offering table is made of birch.
> On this beautiful offering table
> Is golden-red tea.
> The rich offerings in the bowl
> Are as tall as a mountain.
> We offer strong spirits, dark wine
> And a sea of white milk.

Listen to me, hear me well.
There are exactly eighteen
Beautiful small birch trees
Set up for this second-degree *Shanar*.
Listen to me, hear me well.
For offerings to the great clan
There is the *Zalma* Tree.
Listen to me, hear me well.
Om mani padme hum.
This is a great offering
For the Golden White *Serge*
For the great clan
For the gods in the Heavens.
I chant to dedicate
White mother's milk.
I give breath and ask
Listen to me, hear me well.

As Seseg-Abgey chanted, Dulma-Abgey sat beside her. In her left hand Dulma held all the "power flags," small pieces of cloth with drawings of the animals, sun, moon, and other symbols mentioned in the chant. In her right hand she held a bowl of milk. During Seseg's chant she poured the milk on the power flags that were mentioned. This was how she "fed the power animals" and "gave them breath."

Our *Serge*
Stands in the southwestern direction.
On its very top
It has a white ritual cloth.
Listen to me, hear me well.
Om mani padme hum.
The sable power flag flutters in the wind
With its silken tassel
And is a great offering.
I give breath to it and silver it
With white mother's milk.
I chant and give breath to it
Over the smoke of beautiful juniper,

The beautiful juniper that is burning.
Listen to me, hear me well.
Om mani padme hum.
Oh, Ninety-nine Heavens
Nine beautiful *bardags*[1]
Every branch is golden
Every twig is silver
Every bough is cleansed
With white mother's milk.
I give breath and chant
Over burning dark red thyme.
Cleansing, I chant.
Listen to me, hear me well.
Om mani padme hum.
Oh, Golden Yellow Sun,
You make our world golden
Warming us with your rays
Shining your light.
Oh, beloved mother,
I decorate all the tassels on your power flag
So that they will shine like rays.
Feeding them with beautiful mother's milk
I give breath to them and pray
Over red burning thyme.
Cleansing, I chant.
Listen to me, hear me well.
Oh, Silver White Moon,
Our shining father,
You light up the darkness.
Cleansing, I give breath.
Speaking these words, I chant.
Listen to me, hear me well.
Om mani padme hum.
From Ninety-nine Heavens
Come the nine beautiful Sprites.[2]

*Decorating the power
flag of the* Dangenur *or
Nine Sprites*

---

[1] One of the decorations on the tree consisted of nine crumpled pieces
of brocade on a string. These were referred to as the nine *bardags*.
[2] *Dangenur*, or Nine Sprites, carry the offering into the heavens.

I set them running and give them breath.
Cleansing them, I chant.
I cleanse them as they run.
I bring them as an offering
For our beautiful golden *Serge*
For the family tree of the gods in heaven.
Listen to me, hear me well.
Our great offering
Includes five animals[3]
Each is the best of its kind.
Listen to me, hear me well.
I chant to the sound of
My snow-white bell.
I chant as

[3] The five animals mentioned in the chant are: rabbit, stag, black squirrel, kolinsky, and ermine. (The kolinsky is a type of fur-bearing weasel related to the mink.) They are considered to be very swift and nimble animals that can quickly carry the message. The shaman legend given in the sidebar on page 79 refers to them.

Seseg chants as Dulma "feeds" the power flags

The pink and white rabbit runs
I give breath to him as he flies by.
I chant
Cleansing with yellow-red juniper.
Listen to me, hear me well.
Om mani padme hum.
The red stag
Praying, I cleanse
With white mother's milk.
I give it breath and pray
Over the smoke
Of the yellow-red thyme.
I pray and ask.
Listen to me, hear me well.
The nimble black squirrel

Flies through the deep virgin forest.
I cleanse and offer
Dear white milk.
I give breath and ask
Listen to me, hear me well.
Om mani padme hum.
I pray as
The amber-yellow kolinsky
And the nimble white ermine
Race into the heavens.
I offer them white mother's milk
I give breath to them and pray
Over the smoke of
The yellow-red juniper.
Saying the words of the prayer, I ask
Listen to me, hear me well.
Om mani padme hum.
Running between two worlds
They unite
The south and the north side
On the gallop.

Bayir ties the power flags to a birch on the White side

After each power flag was fed, an assistant ran around the grove with it and handed it to Bayir, who tied it to the birch. There were also several three-dimensional objects that were hung or

Five animals

The High Heaven and the Vast Earth decided to become related through marriage. One of the Sons of Heaven was engaged to marry a Daughter of Earth. So Earth asked that Heaven give the Sun and Moon as engagement presents. Heaven could not refuse and delivered the two great bodies of light. The Earth put them in her trunk for safekeeping and a great darkness covered the sky and the land.

High Heaven could not think of a way to get the Sun and the Moon back from the Vast Earth and decided to ask wise Hedgehog for advice. Perhaps together they could come up with a plan to get the Sun and Moon back in the sky. Hedgehog agreed to meet and set out for the heavens. The High Heaven had nine Sons and nine Daughters and strictly forbade them to laugh at Hedgehog. The animal's legs were so short that he didn't walk like the other animals, but rolled like a ball. When Hedgehog entered, the nine Sons and the nine Daughters of Heaven took one look at the funny animal and burst out laughing. Hedgehog was deeply offended and turned to go back home.

So Heaven sent five animals after Hedgehog. They were Rabbit, Deer, Ermine, Squirrel, and Weasel. Heaven told them to follow Hedgehog and listen to what he muttered to himself on the way home. Rabbit first caught up with Hedgehog. He heard the animal say, "Heaven does not know how to control its children. They dared laugh at me. May the Nine Sons and Daughters descend and become spirits. But the problem High Heaven has is easy to solve. Heaven must simply go visit the Vast Earth and ask to be given the echo of the forest and the shimmer of the waters as presents." In Buryat tradition the host gives presents to the guests.

Rabbit reported what he heard to High Heaven. Heaven did exactly what Hedgehog suggested. Then Vast Earth was forced to call her three sons and tell them to capture the echo of the forest and the shimmer of the waters. But no matter how they tried, they failed. So the Vast Earth had to return the Sun and the Moon to High Heaven. Again the two great bodies of light took turns bringing day and night. And Hedgehog's other words also came true. The Nine Sons and Daughters of Heaven descended and became spirits.

— Shaman legend

Seseg blesses the White Guardian with her bardag, *after the offering was accepted*

placed in the branches of the tree. These included the *dakty*, tiny horns of plenty made of birch bark that were filled with butter. Bayir had told us that they fed all three worlds — the Upper, Middle, and Lower Worlds — and united them.

> I pray that the great beautiful meal of
> Seventy-seven horns of plenty
> Filled with beautiful golden butter
> Overflows its rim.
> With white mother's milk
> I give them breath and chant.
> Over the smoke of
> The yellow-red thyme, I cleanse.
> Listen to me, hear me well.

The Upper World includes the sky and the heavens, the Middle World includes all the creatures of the earth, and the Lower World includes the fish in the waters and the creatures that live in the earth. One of the Thunder Songs recorded in this area at the turn of the twentieth century describes this division:

> Every steppe has its own eagle
> Every voice has its own song
> My dear sisters we are
> We are the thunder of the Heavens
>
> Every valley has its own reindeer
> Every throat has its own song
> My dear brothers we are
> We are the thunder of the Heavens
>
> Every stream has its own fish
> Every heart has its own song
> My dear sisters we are
> We are the thunder of the Heavens

Bayir took out a large knife and made four incisions in the base of the birch tree, one for each of the directions of the earth. Then he inserted a red arrowhead, a *zagalme*, into each incision. When I asked him the function of the arrowheads, he said that they sent the sap running up the tree, enlivening it, "giving it breath."

Bayir prepares to make an incision in the birch where he will insert the zagalme, *or red arrowhead*

Bayir places a nest in the branches of the birch

OPPOSITE, ABOVE:
Dulma holds a ball of red thread

OPPOSITE, BELOW:
Bayir tosses the ball of red thread into the ger *through the smoke hole*

Great family tree of the gods in heaven
Thunder and stand at the head
Of this great offering
This beautiful golden *Serge.*
From each of the four directions
The yellow-red arrowheads are inserted.
I pray that they sprout
With white mother's milk.
I give them breath and chant
Over the smoke of
The yellow-red thyme, I cleanse them.
I offer and chant
Listen to me, hear me well.

Bayir also placed three nests on various branches of the birch tree. Each nest contained three golden eggs.

The Great Khan Bird
Flies and cries
Through the Eternal Blue Heaven.
It has three soft nests.
I cleanse them and pray.
Each nest has three eggs.
So I give breath to the nine Golden Eggs
With white mother's milk
And pray.
With pure and beautiful juniper
I cleanse them and pray.
Listen to me, hear me well.

At the foot of the tree were two oil lamps. Vodka bottles that were cut off at the bottom were placed over the lamps to protect the flames.

Blessed and beautiful is the oil lamp
Whose light and rays scatter.
I cleanse it and give breath to it

With mother's white milk.
Listen to me, hear me well.

The shamans placed a small wooden statue of a camel at the foot of the birch. Bayir tied a red thread around its neck and then tied the red thread to the very top of the *Serge* or Hitching Post Tree. Then the assistants tied the thread around each of the eighteen birch saplings and the *Zalma* or Offering Tree at the other end of the southern grove. Bayir took the ball of red thread and tossed it through the round smoke hole at the top of the *ger*. His assistants caught the ball of thread inside. They wound it through the support poles and let it descend to the center altar set up on the north side of the *ger*. Bayir said that the spirits would descend down the red thread to the *Serge*, through the saplings and the *Zalma* Tree to the altar. If for some reason they moved down the

other end of the thread they would sit on the camel and their feet would never touch the ground.

> The young camel with the silver harness
> Transports
> The family tree of the gods.
> I give it breath so that it blossoms
> And flies up over the red thread.
> Descend on the red thread
> From the Golden *Serge*
> Through each of the eighteen
> Delicate beautiful young birches.
> Make a circle
> And descend through the *Zalma* Tree
> Without any mistakes.
> Enter with a prayer
> Into the white round tent
> According to the Golden Sun
> Through the smoke hole
> To our golden-yellow oil-lamp.
> Descend without any mistakes.
> Oh, great family tree of the gods in heaven
> Listen to me and look after this ritual.

Then, in a very similar ceremony, Dulma-Abgey "gave life to the trees" on the Black side. Bayir told me that the order of the five animals is slightly different on the Black side. Afterwards, the Guardian of the Ritual on the Black side put the milk that was part of the ritual on Dulma's drum. He knelt under the drum as Dulma chanted and then she tossed the cup with the milk. If the cup fell right side up, the spirits accepted the offering. The Guardian of the Ritual ran to the cup that sat right side up in the grass. He made three circles around it "according to the sun," knelt, lifted the cup to his lips, and drank the remains. Dulma then blessed her Guardian of the Ritual. The spirits had accepted the offering of the birches.

Now food could be offered to the spirits. The Buryat Aga Region was traditionally a herding society, and to this day food here means either milk or meat. Eastern Buryats did not practice

agriculture and felt it was a sin to plow and disturb the earth. This made ecological sense in this steppe region. The growing season is too short and the soil too thin for agriculture. Even today most people in the Buryat Aga Region raise their own sheep and eat meat at almost every meal. If you want to eat here, you learn to help slaughter the animals.

Dambakha, the man who would slaughter the sheep, and the two women who would dress the meat entered the *ger*. Bayir addressed them: "We — me, you Dambakha, and you two ladies — have to make an agreement with the Father, Mother, the Nine Children, the two Guardians, the two Cupbearers, seven living breaths in Volodya's family,[4] and the twelve families that live in Chelutay. In order for their children to live long and well, the four of us have to sin. To simply kill a sheep is not a sin. But if we kill the sheep and I cannot send its soul to the Thirteen Northern Spirits, it will be my sin and my fault. You, Dambakha, if you make the sheep suffer, if you make it cry, or break its bone, or fail to find its artery or lose the *iltahan*, the ritual metal human figure, it will be your sin and your fault. You two women who will dress the sheep, if you let one hair fall, or mix the blood with the undigested food,

LEFT: *Dulma chants as Seseg "feeds" the power flags*

RIGHT: *Dulma prepares to toss the cup to see if the offering was accepted, as the Black Guardian kneels under her drum*

---

[4] Bayir means the seven living members of Volodya's immediate family, the two parents and the five children.

OPPOSITE ABOVE LEFT:
*Dulma gives milk for
the sheep to drink*

OPPOSITE ABOVE
RIGHT: *Dambakha
breaks the artery*

it will be your fault. Many shamans have died because of mistakes in the ritual with the sheep. I am not a great shaman; I have just started on this path. I don't want to die because of you. I have five children. I tell you this — I will fulfill my task completely. But you should make sure that not a single drop of sweat or a single drop of human blood falls on the meat of this sheep. The fleece of this sheep should not get dirty. Everything should be done cleanly. We are preparing an offering for Volodya's ancestor who should descend from the White Heavens. This offering is for him. We should be responsible, not lose our nerve, be clean and do everything according to tradition.

"Now, did you offer up your *hadaks*?" Bayir asked them. "What did you say? I didn't hear. You offered up the *hadaks* in a ritual, didn't you?" The women and Dambakha said yes and Bayir continued. "If you did something incorrectly, it will be your fault. Don't hold us responsible. If in the coming year you get sick or die. . . . You, Mother and Father, are you listening? And you two Guardians, Cupbearers, and Nine Children, are you all listening? Everyone should assume responsibility for their own actions. Do you want to die because of me?" When everyone in the *ger* said no, Bayir said, "If you die, I don't want to follow in your footsteps."

Bayir then asked for the *iltahan*. This turned out to be a piece of metal cut out in the shape of a man. He wrapped the form in sheep's wool and said, "Look: this is a human figure. We will give it to the man who will slaughter the sheep. We do this to find out Volodya's fate and how Volodya will die. From where it winds up in the sheep, we will be able to tell whether he will go insane, or

die because of arm or leg injuries, or have an accident, or die in the steppe. Perhaps Volodya will live long, become an old man and die of old age. That would be best." Then Bayir told Dambakha, "You must hold the *iltahan* in your right hand with three fingers like so."

The sheep was brought in and Bayir started to beat his drum and chant to the Thirteen Northern Spirits. The sheep started breathing in rhythm to Bayir's drum. As the rhythm of the drum picked up so did its breath. Dulma spread butter on the sheep's hooves, sprinkled the sheep with vodka three times. Then she tied a strip of cloth on the sheep's back. They made the sheep kneel and Bayir drummed right over the sheep. Dulma gave the sheep milk to drink and the sheep drank it. The sheep was turned over, milk was spread on its chest. Then in one swift movement Dambakha made a small cut, stuck his arm into the sheep's chest, and broke the main artery. At the same time he inserted the *iltahan*. Later when the meat was dressed they couldn't find the *iltahan* at first. Dambakha said that the metal figure was too large and did not fit under the main artery along the spine. When they finally found it, the form was bent on the left side. Bayir said this meant that Volodya would die accidentally because of an injury to his left leg.

The iltahan, *or ritual metal human figure*

PART II

CALLING THE SPIRITS

Great ancestors of my family tree
Descend and thunder

The Ongon Spirits

"For a shaman, nothing on earth is eternal," Bayir said. "This land is not ours forever. We descend here for a given time and then we depart. Why do we chant and shamanize? Our ancestors are eternal. We appeal to our ancestors, to our family tree on both the father and mother's side. Seseg, Dulma, and I work with people's fates and we understand this."

The spirits that the shamans called down at the *Shanar* are called *ongons*. They are the spirits of respected individuals who have died. Many of them had once been famous shamans. Bayir told us that when a spirit comes down, he first comes to the place where his body was buried and from that point goes to the place where he is being called.

At a *Shanar* the spirits come to the *Serge* Tree and travel on the red thread through all the trees, then come to the Offering Tree under which the meat stands. From there the spirit can travel on the red thread to the altar in the *ger*.

The spirit appears to be the age at which he died and his disposition depends on his death. If he died violently, he comes full of anger. If he died peacefully and was able to come to terms with his death, he will be kind and gentle.

"The spirit comes to the feet first," Bayir said. "When I am being inhabited I change from the inside out, from the bone out. I change totally. I am forty, but when a 103-year-old spirit enters me, my face, my entire body, changes drastically."

At the ritual we saw Bayir call down a number of spirits. He always started by chanting and beating his drum. He picked up the rhythm several times and brought it back down. Then he increased the rhythm to a feverous pitch before throwing his drum aside. Suddenly he was standing, trembling and jumping. When the spirit entered him, his entire body changed to assume the posture of the

spirit. The people who had gathered scrambled to stand and cover their eyes, holding the tips of their fingers to their brows. The assistants followed the spirit, who walked around and often headed into the birch grove. They would try to get the spirit to sit on the *olbok*, a traditional brocade pillow, and accept tea or tobacco. If the spirit was angry, he would refuse to be placated for a long time.

Once the spirit sat down and accepted anything that was offered, one of the assistants, called a *khelemershen*, would speak with the spirit. During the *Shanar* Dulma often filled this role. She would always have a piece of paper with questions for the spirit. The spirit answered through Bayir's body, but it did not sound like his voice. Dulma would also write down the answers. Later all the shamans would gather to interpret the meaning and the implications of these statements.

A shaman's special knowledge comes from his contact with the spirits, especially the spirits of his own ancestors. Bayir had told us, "With the power of my drum I can take my own spirit out of my body. When my spirit is in this state I can communicate with my ancestors, with one of the shamans from the twelve generations on my father's side or the seven generations on my mother's side. I learn about shamanism from them. Only my father and his father died early; my other ancestors all lived to a ripe old age and had many *Shanars*. The power of these generations has helped me understand many things and cure gravely ill people."

> BAYIR: *Tuyana, did you see how Harme's spirit came into me?*
>
> TUYANA: *No, I was standing on the wrong side.*
>
> BAYIR: *I told you many times that the male spirits enter from one direction and female ones come from the other side. You must learn to see them. Some spirits enter as if they were coming from under a pile of rocks. The rocks fall away and the* ongon *rises. Then it enters you in a rush. Other spirits come bouncing in like a ball. Before you go to sleep you should stare at a lightbulb. Then close your eyes and learn to move the light in your mind from left to right. You can also practice making it disappear.*
>
> TUYANA: *You've told me this before. I've been trying to do this exercise. Each night I stare at the bulb till my eyes hurt. But I can't get it to move. I only wind up crying from frustration. (Everyone laughs.)*
>
> BAYIR: *When I call down Harme Zarin I see sparks at first. My ancestor Khukheron Boo appears very differently. He arrives with a lot of loud noise. He enters as a large man, who was shot in 1929. He is harsh and appears with a frightening scream. He wants to grasp everything, see everything. He is very strong. If there are problems, we will call him.*

The spirits that descended at the *Shanar* were very much people of their own times. They spoke an old form of Buryat and were most comfortable in traditional surroundings. That is why the petitioners sometimes went to great lengths to set up the tent just right, or to make some traditional dish that the spirit would recognize. Sometimes a spirit asked for an ancient song or treat no longer made in the region. If these simple requests could not be met, it could send the whole ritual off in a different direction.

One of the spirits Bayir called down several times was Harme Zarin.[1] He is a very old man who has no teeth.

---

[1] *Zarin* is the title of a shaman with the highest rank who has completed all the *Shanar* rituals. Today there is only one living *Zarin*.

DULMA: It's very hard to understand what Harme Zarin says.

PROFESSOR MARGARITA: Maybe you can listen to this recording I made, Bayir-Akhe?

BAYIR: I wouldn't understand it anyway. Only Dulma and Seseg understand him.

SESEG: No, not me, I really don't understand a word of what Harme Zarin says.

DULMA: He is very patient with me. He always asks, "Did you understand?" When I say no, he starts to explain everything from the very beginning. (Everyone laughed.)

SAYAN: At a ritual we attended before this an *ongon* came and touched a woman's head. They had put her head under his hand so he could bless her. But he kept touching and touching her hair. Then suddenly he asked, "What's wrong with her? Where are her braids?" (Everyone laughed.)

BAYIR: That's nothing. Dulma, do you remember what Harme Zarin said last time we called him down?

DULMA: We asked about this nineteen-year-old girl, and Harme Zarin asked if she was married. When we said no, he said, "What kind of girl are you asking about if no goat or bull wants her? What an ancient old maid!"

SESEG: In those days they used to get married when they were fourteen years old. So someone who was unmarried at nineteen was an ancient old maid, indeed.

BAYIR: But I've got to admit that our granddad, Harme Zarin, is always absolutely right about everything he says. I've been calling him down for years. And when I compare him to all the other *ongons*, I see that he is always very exact about what he says.

Another *ongon* Bayir often calls down is Khukheron Boo. He is one of Bayir's relatives. "Khukheron Boo is no Harme," Bayir once told us. "He can be real tough. Once when an initiation ritual for a shaman was not working out, Khukheron Boo was called. 'Listen,' he said, 'bury this guy. Put a gravestone over his head and pick someone else for this ritual.' And the people were obliged to find another candidate for the initiation because once a ritual is started it must be completed."

Tuyana told us that something similar had actually happened to her. She was very sick and had come to a ritual that was being

Volodya offers an olbok, or traditional brocade pillow, to the ongon

done for another shaman. The spirits were not happy with the shaman who was being dedicated and they told the shamans to find another candidate. Much to her surprise, the shamans chose Tuyana.

Bayir told many stories about Khukheron Boo during the *Shanar*. "I did a ritual for someone and we called down one of his ancient ancestors. Long ago when this ancestor was doing a ritual for a sixteen-year-old girl, he drank too much vodka and let the girl's soul escape. So the girl died. This was all long, long ago, but one day when I was doing this ritual for one of his descendants the spirit of this offended girl comes to the ritual and prevents it from going smoothly. So, we called down Khukheron Boo. He starts yelling at me, saying, 'What kind of shaman are you, if you are afraid of a sixteen-year-old girl. I'll take her aside and you . . . you continue with your ritual.' He is very harsh, but fair. He is not one to pity people. He tells you the hard truth, just like it is. If you are fated to die tomorrow, he will tell you. But he will also take off his

Dulma, as the khelemershen, *speaks with the* ongon

shoes and run over hot coals in order to do a cleansing ritual for you."

Sayan reminded Bayir of another story about Khukheron Boo. "Oh, yes," Bayir said, "that was in Sahata. Many years ago children started dying there. The elders called in various shamans to do all kinds of rituals, but nothing helped. Then they invited

The ongon *accepts the drink that is offered*

Ongon in birch grove

Khukheron Boo. He arrived a little drunk. He entered the tent and slept for two days. The people who had gathered for the ritual started to wander off. 'Who was this man,' they thought, 'a serious shaman or a drunk?' Then he awoke and said, 'Bring me the skin of an otter.' He took the skin and put it into a trough filled with water. He covered the trough and said, 'When something stirs in the trough, wake me.' For three days he drank and again the people began to leave. Suddenly, someone noticed something stirring in the trough. They woke Khukheron Boo. He had them uncover the trough. Inside, they found a live otter swimming in the water. Khukheron Boo offered the otter to the spirits, asking them to protect the children. This was seventy years ago and for seventy years they were protected. Now, once again, things are not well there."

"In Kunkur," Bayir told us, "there is an old man who was one of the Children of Heaven at Khukheron Boo's *Shanar*. This ninety-year-old elder believes that he is alive to this day because he was part of Khukheron Boo's ritual. All his brothers, both older and younger, have died long ago."

But not all stories we heard about Khukheron Boo had unexpectedly happy endings. At the end of the 1920s the government started to persecute shamans. Bayir told us that Khukheron Boo was arrested several times then, but the authorities could never hold him. They would lock him up in the local prison, but by the next morning he would always disappear. Only when they arrested his family did Khukheron Boo finally appear before the authorities. He came voluntarily and was then sent to Krasny Yar near Chita, where he was executed. Bayir told us that Khukheron Boo said he would erase to the root the clan of the man who denounced him to the Secret Police and, apparently, there are no living survivors.

Bayir also told us the following story: "One day I was driving to town and saw an old woman named Dulma standing by the side of the road, looking for a ride. I was alone, so I gave her a ride. She gets in and tells me, 'I had three *Altan Serge* Rituals.[1] I made offerings to a man from Cold Valley who could turn himself into a blue wolf.' I say, 'that's nice,' but I can tell she wants to say something to me. Then she says, 'Who do you make offerings to?' I said, 'My grandfather. I only make offerings to my grandfather.' She looked at me for a long time and then asked, 'Do you make offerings to Khukheron Boo?' So I said, 'Who is he?'" Everyone laughed, since they knew Bayir made offerings to Khukheron Boo. Then Bayir continued, "She looked at me again for a long time and said, 'I know you make offerings to Khukheron Boo. I heard about it from other people.' So I told her the truth: 'Yes, I make offerings to Khukheron Boo.' She started to cry and said, 'Late one night many years ago when Khukheron Boo was arrested someone brought me his ritual objects. When the man placed the ritual objects on the northwest side, there was a sign. A strong wind blew four times from the west. After that the man said, "These ritual objects have a prophecy attached to them. In the future a young man will grow up here who should take these ritual objects."' That is what grandma Dulma said to me."

---

[1] *Altan Serge* Rituals are the first rituals an individual undergoes before they have a *Shanar* and become a shaman.

Great, uh . . . ancestors . . . of my family tree,
Listen to me . . . hear me well.
(Volodya: What comes next?)

The Fading Light of a Golden Afternoon

The ritual was going very smoothly, we concluded, as we reviewed the events so far. The previous day the trees had been prepared, the participants cleansed, and the sacred grounds sealed. That morning the souls of the participants had been sent to the Spirits of the Baikal, the trees had been "given breath," and the meat was offered. The offerings were all accepted. We were looking forward to the most important part of the ritual, the descent of the *ongons*.

In the *ger*, Volodya, the new shaman, sat down in front of the altar to chant to his ancestor spirits. He was dressed in his new White shaman's cape and handed his bell. The Children of Heaven started chanting the White refrain: *"Padme hum om mani."* Then

Volodya started his first chant. He stumbled through every line and couldn't fall into a rhythm with the bell. Tuyana and Bato-Bolot, the two assistant shamans who were his friends, sat next to him, trying to help him and lend their moral support. Tuyana, very precise in her own chants, started prompting Volodya.

For the, uh . . . beautiful Golden Shanar
I call you, uh . . . with the song of my, uh . . . ringing bell
And, uh . . . chant.
(Volodya: What comes next?
Tuyana, prompting him: From the beautiful Golden
    Serge. . . .
Volodya: Oh, yeah.) From the beautiful. . . .

When Volodya paused, discouraged, Tuyana scrambled and sat down next to him. She reviewed the next section of the chant with him and encouraged him. Volodya launched into the chant, but then started stumbling again. Soon he was only ringing his bell, and Bato-Bolot prompted him. Eventually, with a lot of help, Volodya got through the chant on the White side. It did not feel like he had made contact with his ancestor spirits.

After a short break Bato-Bolot told the Guardian of the Ritual to get Volodya's drum ready. The Children of Heaven started to chant the Black refrain as Volodya was dressed. Volodya started to chant and beat his drum, but soon stopped. Tuyana encouraged him and Volodya started beating his drum again. But his rhythm was unsteady. Tired, Tuyana took off her glasses, wiped her brow, and looked to Bato-Bolot for help.

Seseg walked in to check how things were going. The three leading shamans, Bayir, Seseg, and Dulma, had withdrawn when Volodya readied to make his first attempt at chanting. Perhaps they did not want to intimidate him with their presence. Seseg now walked up to Volodya and placed her hand on his back. She listened for a minute, then fiddled with the metal disc on the back of his robe. Finally, she handed Tuyana some wooden cups and withdrew again. Tuyana started mouthing all the words of the chant, hoping this would help her friend. Volodya managed to complete the Black chant.

Bayir, Seseg, and Dulma returned to evaluate the situation. "Volodya, when you were asleep," Bayir asked, "what kind of dream did you have? Did you feel anything when you were calling down the *ongon*? Did anything touch you?" Volodya looked downcast. He just shook his head no.

Slowly, Bayir started to dress and get ready to chant. "We shouldn't rush things," he said. "There is a time for everything.

There is a moment during the *Shanar* when the spirits descend, when the *ongons* come. That is why it is important that the Children of Heaven always be ready to help the new shaman. Seseg, Dulma, and I cannot make Volodya do anything. We can only listen to what his ancestors say. If they say let him run up the tree, then we will do so. If they say no, then we will not. The moment will come when Volodya will run up the tree, when he will lose his reason and start to cry. The weight of his body will disappear. Once the spirits of the White Heavens enter him, he will be able to lick hot iron or walk over burning coals. He will be able to take out a person's soul and effortlessly lift their body. Or he can have his horse run over the surface of a lake, or cross the mighty Onon River.

"I don't know what the *ongon* will say," Bayir continued. "An argument or a tug-of-war can arise between the in-laws. Two great in-laws, two great shamans ordered the same outfit. This is already a bad sign. Volodya had a dream in which three arrows fell. Outsiders say something is coming from the south. So, we don't know what will happen. We don't know how many nights we will have to spend here. That's what we think now."

PROFESSOR MARGARITA: Well, you better give the rest of us some protection, too.

SAYAN: We are protected. We have been cleansed like the others.

PROFESSOR MARGARITA: It's all becoming more and more frightening.

SESEG: Don't go outside the sacred ritual grounds.

BAYIR: We have put trees to the Four Directions. This is for the fifty-five Western Heavens and the fifty Masters of the Mountains and the five protectors. We have pulled out mountain trees at the root, cut mountain trees at their roots, and decorated them with white and blue ritual cloths. We have a birch *Serge*, a golden *Zalma* tree, and a birch altar with four offerings of traditional white food. All these are protecting you. The great spirits of the North, South, West, and East protect our *Shanar*. We have also made an altar for the local spirits of Chelutay. Inside the sacred grounds you are protected, but once you step outside something can happen. Yesterday I warned you not to walk around alone, especially at dawn or dusk.

Then Bayir chanted and called down the first *ongon*. Bayir beat his drum very quickly, jumped up, and the spirit entered him. It was Harme Zarin, who tended to explain things carefully but could be difficult to understand. Dulma spoke with the spirit and addressed him as "Babey," a respectful term for a father. She first introduced Volodya to the spirit and then started to inquire about the problems.

DULMA: Babey, the *Shanar's* shaman is named Volodya. He is forty-seven and from the Mondon Khargana clan. Please check to see how the *Shanar* is going.

(HARME ZARIN said something that ended with, "there is a lot to grasp.")

DULMA: His ancestors ordered a special cape with many small snakes. How are we to understand this?

(HARME said something.)

DULMA: Then we should listen to what both sides say and do what they say without deciding. Yes?

HARME: Don't decide, listen to both sides, but listen to the soft side more, the side of the mother.

DULMA: Thank you. Babey, please help us from your side with this matter. Please be our guardian.

Then the spirit left Bayir. He jumped up and down, round and round according to the sun. He shook and trembled. An assistant held him, as another placed a stool for him to sit on and took off his headdress. A third wiped his face and massaged his hands. The Guardian of the Ritual circled him with sacred smoke.

"So what did the spirit say?" Bayir asked. "That there is much to grasp," answered Dulma. There was a long pause, as everyone realized there would be many problems they would have to grasp and solve before the ritual could end. "He also said," Dulma continued, "that we should start calling on the soft side and listen to what those spirits say." The Buryats call their female ancestor line the soft side.

Then there was a long discussion as the shamans tried to clarify what Volodya's heritage could be on the soft side. Was the spirit referring to his mother's side or his grandmother on his father's side? They asked Volodya what was said to him at his first *Shanar*. Volodya was unsure; he also did not seem to know all the details of his own heritage on his mother's side.

This was odd, since most Buryats tend to know a great deal about their own heritage. People can recite the names of their ancestors going back seven generations. Many people have copies of their clan book, which tells the story of their family from mythic times through all the generations to the present. Shamans, in particular, learn all the details of their family history because they need to know them when dealing with their ancestor spirits. But for some reason Volodya was vague on these important details.

Bayir then decided to call down another spirit — Manzhiley, who is the Master of the *Shanar* Ritual. "I will do Manzhiley," Bayir said. "Is everything ready?" But Volodya seemed more interested in mundane matters. "We were going to eat dinner," he reminded Bayir. "Oh, yes, we've got to eat," Bayir said, and added, "Listen, when we do Manzhiley don't choke me or drop me." Everyone

The shamans confer

laughed. "You laugh," Bayir continued, "but it hurts me. Do you remember, Professor Margarita, the ritual we did in Moscow? There was this man who was supposed to catch me, but instead he started hopping with me as if he was the one who was going into *ongon*." "Oh, yes," Dulma remembered. "I yelled, 'Hold him. Hold him.' And he yells back, 'Who? Who?'" Again, everyone laughed.

The shamans warned all the people who had gathered at the edge of the sacred grounds about Manzhiley. The people were told to cover their eyes and to stay far back. Manzhiley is a very aggressive spirit. Long ago he was a shaman and the son of a great khan. But he died unexpectedly when he was only twenty-eight, so when he arrives he is very angry.

Women gathered at the edge of the sacred grounds

The Guardian of the Ritual lit the oil lamps in the northern grove. Bayir put on the *orgay* for the first time during this ritual and started to chant. Then suddenly Manzhiley entered him. The *ongon* said little. "The problem has nothing to do with me," he said. "It concerns your own ancestors." He ran through the birch grove, where the terrified Mother and Father blurted out their introductions. When Dulma tried to introduce

Shaman chanting in orgay

Volodya, Manzhiley ran to the Children of Heaven. They tried to get him to sit and drink tea, but he refused. He yelled at Volodya and hit his back with the *bardag*, and ran toward the women who were helping in the kitchen. There Manzhiley made a motion with his *bardag* and some women ran off scared, thinking he would hit them. As a result an old woman was pushed and cut her forehead against the horns of the *orgay*. Then, just as suddenly as he came, Manzhiley left Bayir.

Seseg walked over to the women to see who was hurt. It was one of Volodya's elderly relatives. The wound turned out to be a simple scratch. Seseg asked if Manzhiley had said something to them. The women answered, "Yes, but we didn't understand what he said." Seseg explained that he probably wanted to bless them with the *bardag* when the panic broke out and the grandmother was hurt.

The shamans laughed about the reactions of the Mother and Father to Manzhiley. They said that once Manzhiley scared a Mother at a ritual so much that when he asked her to name her

clan the poor woman froze with terror. When they prodded her
for an answer, she looked at the meat in front of her and said,
"Sheep." Everyone laughed. Then they asked the Mother of this
ritual if she too was of the "Sheep" clan. Again, everyone laughed.

Bayir decided to heed the advice of Harme Zarin and first call
down Volodya's relative on the "soft side." Buzhagar Babey was
Volodya's ancestor on his grandfather's mother's side. This meant
that this spirit was not strictly related to Volodya according to one
gender line, which the Buryat shamans considered to be very
important, but Volodya had always made offerings to this spirit.
Bayir had told us previously that Buzhagar Babey wanted to leave
this world, but before he could leave Volodya would have to rise in
rank as a shaman. Then Volodya could protect his own clan without relying on Buzhagar Babey's special protection. The spirit also
told Volodya to listen only to him, and not call down other spirits.
However, one day Volodya had a dream in which Zandan Zarin

The ongon *enters the*
shaman

came to him. He told Bayir about this dream, and Bayir told Volodya that Zandan was his direct relative, since he was his relative on his grandfather's father side. After this, Volodya started to make offerings to both spirits. In his first chant at this ritual Volodya had actually mentioned both spirits.

Buzhagar Bural Babey[1]
Your homeland is Khuhan Khereta
You come from the Boro Tolre
You fly in the Blue Heavens.

Zandan Bural Babey[2]
Is from the far southeast
From the locality of Khure Khile.
His family tree is the birch.

Volodya probably hoped that in making an offering to two great ancestors he would receive double protection. Instead he was creating a problem for himself.

It was getting to be late in the day. The sun had set and the light was fading fast. Bayir dressed again in his *orgay* and started chanting. When Buzhagar Babey entered Bayir, Dulma introduced Volodya to the spirit. Volodya knelt down and bowed before him. The *ongon* felt Volodya's back with his left hand. He asked that Volodya's *orgay* be brought. He looked at them and said something about coming back with the red sunrise next day. He told Dulma to look for an eagle in the sky. The reason he chose an eagle as his omen was not coincidental. The *dudalga*, the words one had to say to call down this spirit, were "Eagle Buzhagar Babey."

The shamans had anticipated trouble with Volodya's ancestors. Now, although Volodya failed to contact his ancestors directly, Bayir had managed to call down one of them. Buzhagar Babey, Volodya's ancestor on his soft side, said he would come back to help Volodya the next day. Everyone relaxed. Bayir, Dulma, and Seseg retreated to help some of the outsiders who needed healing. The other participants headed off to sleep.

---

[1] Buzhagar is his name. Bural Babey means "Gray-Haired Father."
[2] Zandan means "sandalwood" and is his name.

The Fog Rolls In

Next morning the sunrise lit up the clouds a rich rosy red, but then a heavy, milky fog descended on the sacred grounds. I got up early and met Tuyana as she was washing up. We had tea and she asked me to redo her bandage. She hissed when I touched the cut with an alcohol wipe and I bit my lip, but the jagged cut across her palm did not seem as raw. I also noticed that Tuyana could now curl her fingers and took this as a positive sign.

Tuyana told me that Bayir had decided to put off the ritual until after the fog cleared. As the fog lifted at noon everyone gathered to look for a sign. The Children of Heaven stood near the grove holding Volodya's ritual objects, while the shamans conferred and waited for a sign.

Then Bayir started to get ready to chant. Dulma checked the offerings. Fresh vodka and milk were poured. Broken twigs on the offered birches were cleaned and anointed with butter. The Guardian of the Ritual circled the north grove with sacred smoke. Since Harme Zarin had advised the shamans to speak to both sides, Bayir decided to now call down Zandan Babey, Volodya's relative on his male side. He asked for the words that would call down Zandan Babey. An assistant shaman brought Bayir's *orgay* and held the shaman's horns over sacred smoke.

The Children of Heaven chanted the Black refrain: *Ahe-yohe mini go/Ai don baydgo mini go.* They circled the birch trees, carrying the ritual objects. One of the girls beat the drum in time. Bayir put on the shaman's horns and started to chant. Suddenly he stopped. The drum sounded flat. Bayir asked that his assistant dry it again. As we waited for the drum, the shamans smoked and lit a pipe just in case the *ongon* asked for one. Then they dressed Bayir again and his assistant handed him the reheated drum. Bayir started the chant to Volodya's ancestor. Although Volodya sat right next to Bayir, he was obviously not really paying attention. Even the leader of the Children of Heaven seemed more attentive.

As the *ongon* of Zandan Babey entered Bayir, two eagles appeared in the sky. The *ongon* went into the birch trees and paced

next to the offering. Dulma spoke with the *ongon* and started by introducing Volodya.

DULMA: Zandan Bural Babey, Volodya is from the beautiful clan of Khargana. He is forty-seven years old. He was born in the Year of the Beautiful Horse. Mountain trees were pulled out with their roots. Mountain trees were cut at the root. He offers you a complete golden *Shanar*, which has a Father and Mother, nine beautiful Children of Heaven, two beautiful Guardians of the Ritual, and two beautiful Cupbearers. Babey, we have placed a brocade pillow behind you. Please be so kind and sit down. (Then she turned briskly to the Mother.) Mother of our beautiful golden *Shanar*, please introduce yourself.

OKTIABRINA: I'm from the Galzud clan. Our clan password is "Young Colt." I'm called Oktiabrina. I am thirty-six years old and was born in the Year of the Snake. I am the Mother of this Golden *Shanar*.

DULMA: (briskly) Father of the *Shanar*, come here!

BATOMUNKO: The Father is from the Khubdud clan. Our clan password is "Black Eagle." I am called Batomunko. I was born in the Year of the Dragon. I am the Father of this Golden *Shanar*.

DULMA: This *Shanar* has a Father and a Mother, nine beautiful Children of Heaven, two beautiful

Guardians of the Ritual, and two beautiful Cupbearers. Please sit down. Have pity on us. Please sit down.

(Zandan did not respond but was breathing heavily and groaned.)

Dulma: Babey, please accept our yellow-red tea and drink it. (Dulma then repeated the introductions.) Please drink the tea.

(Zandan did not respond, but groaned. The air hummed with the flies that gathered on the offered meat. Then the *ongon* spoke very slowly and unclearly.)

Dulma: Babey, we placed a night guard who kept an eye on our *Shanar* all night. But it is possible that cows or dogs were here and took something.

(Zandan said something inaudible and touched the right knee bone of the offered meat.)

Dulma: We are late,[1] dear children. We have not seen terrible events, we have not heard horrible cries. The sun is turned towards us. We are taking our first steps. Please forgive our mistakes.

(Zandan spoke for a long time, but it was inaudible.)

Dulma: (nodded) Yes. Yes. Yes. (Suddenly there was a strong gust of wind and the offering trees swayed. The leaves rustled in the

[1] A "late" child means one of the latest or most recent generation.

wind.) Bring Volodya. (Volodya fell on his knees in front of the *ongon*.)

VOLODYA: Babey, I have four sons on whom I can lean. I also have one daughter.

(ZANDAN said something. They called Volodya's wife, who knelt in front of the *ongon*.)

VOLODYA: This is my wife. She was born in the Year of the Pig.

(ZANDAN said a blessing. Then he said a blessing over Dulma.)

DULMA: (introducing Seseg) The leader of the White side is from the Bodongud clan, from the beautiful Chandali. She is called Seseg. She is forty-seven years old, born in the Year of the Horse.

Zandan hit Seseg with the *bardag* and blessed her. Then the Children of Heaven approached him. They all introduced themselves, saying their clan and names. The spirit blessed all of them and the Children of Heaven responded, "May it be so." Then the *ongon* left Bayir. He jumped up and down, turning round and round. The assistants held him. The Guardian circled him with sacred smoke. They took off the *orgay* and gave Bayir a stool.

The shamans gathered to decipher what the spirit said. Seseg told Bayir that the spirit had blessed the leaders of the Black and White sides. He then had blessed the Nine Children of Heaven, the two Guardians of the Ritual, and the Cupbearers. He had also blessed the Father and Mother of the Ritual and wished them all ninety-nine years.

BAYIR: Did he bless me? (Everyone laughed.) Dulma, I bet you grabbed my blessing, didn't you?[2]

DULMA: Yes, I admit it. I'd split it with you, but I'm not sure which part I should give you. (Everyone laughed.)

BAYIR: What did the spirit say?

DULMA: He told me, "Three years from now at this man's next *Shanar* you will be the leader the Black side. Help him."

SESEG: When he blessed me, he said, "May everything be well in your homeland with people's fates."

---

[2] Bayir was actually the leader of the Black side at the *Shanar*.

Ongon *near the meat offering*

DULMA: Zandan said, "I wanted to have him run up the Father Tree, but a spirit from the mother's side, Buzhagar Babey, came and said, "I will run him up the Mother Tree."

BAYIR: The Mother Tree?

VOLODYA: Buzhagar Babey is my ancestor on my grandfather's mother's side. But Zandan Babey is my ancestor on my grandfather's father's side.

DULMA: The spirit said, "We found a common language and made an agreement. Volodya will complete three *Shanars*." He said, "This *Shanar* will be Buzhagar Babey's. I will let him go first." But he was a bit angry and as soon as he came, two eagles appeared in the sky. One was way up high in the sky, the other a little lower.

SESEG: I made an offering of wheat grains then.

DULMA: Zandan Babey told me, "I sent a thick fog to interfere with your *Shanar*." But then he said he would help Volodya run up the tree. "Raise the offering with the red sun of the evening. I will correct the mistakes in your *Shanar's* meat offering and raise it."

BAYIR: I'm glad he said that. I was afraid there might be mistakes.

DULMA: He said, "My time will come. Three years from now I will help him and there will be no mistakes. What you don't know, you don't know, but don't forget what you've learned. Don't talk unnecessarily. Three years after the third *Shanar* do a special Ritual with the Red Horse.

BAYIR: Does he have a limp?

DULMA: Yes. He kept on touching his right leg.

VOLODYA: They say he fell off a horse and hurt his leg.

DULMA: He also said, "Think before you speak at a sacred place."

BAYIR: I wonder why he said that?

VOLODYA: Probably because he had made that mistake himself.

TUYANA: Zandan's relatives speak and a river of words flows. Remember, Volodya, don't say anything unnecessary.

DULMA: He said, "Worship the Master of the family tree. Pray to the northern stars for harvest. Do a Ritual of Offering in the spring when the trees bloom and in the autumn when the leaves fall."

BAYIR: Dulma, you've become a veritable font of information.

DULMA: Yes, but little of it remains in my head. When there is too much information, much of it gets lost. Oh, by the way, the spirit also said that the *Zalma*, or Offering Tree, should be raised on a red horse to the northwest.

BAYIR: The northwest? That means we will be raising it to Buzhagar Babey. I'm amazed that Zandan let him go first.

DULMA: He said, "We found a common language."

BAYIR: In that case, let's try to call the *ongon* of Buzhagar Babey.

DULMA: He also said, "I am glad you waited till the fog cleared."

SESEG: I knew there was a good reason why I slept so late. (Everyone laughed.)

BAYIR: Well, then we will call Buzhagar Babey himself.

Everyone was relieved since it seemed that a major problem had been resolved. Zandan Babey had said he would step aside for Buzhagar Bural Babey. He would allow Volodya to raise this *Shanar* to Buzhagar Bural Babey. The tug-of-war between the two great ancestors was now surely over.

"Now we will call down Volodya's ancestor Buzhagar Babey," Bayir said, "and we will talk to him again. He had said that he would come to us again with the red sunrise. 'If you hear a bird call or see an eagle from the south side, don't go anywhere till the afternoon sun, wait here.' When we awoke there was a heavy fog. We were afraid we would not be able to see signs from heaven, so we waited till the fog cleared. Otherwise we would have started the ritual long ago. Yesterday the *ongon* said, 'Run my boy up the tree.' If Buzhagar Babey comes again and says the same thing, we will make Volodya run. If he runs up the tree, we should take him down quickly and make an offering on the Black side and then quickly move to the White side. The spirit should hit you in the back, Volodya; free you from the weight of your body. We will see which tree Volodya will climb, the Father Tree or the Mother Tree. This is very important."

Now the sun was shining and everything took on a positive glow. But as the events unfolded, our optimism at this moment proved an illusion. The problems with Volodya and the *ongons* were just beginning. It soon became evident that the old spirit of Harme Zarin had been right when he said that "there was much to grasp."

The shamans decided that it was time for Volodya to call down Buzhagar Babey, the *ongon* to whom he had always made offerings. Volodya was dressed. His outfit was new and extravagant. He had a beautiful set of *orgay* with eagle feathers. But he started drumming badly and his *orgay* were soon taken off. Bayir listened to Volodya drum for a little bit and suggested a rhythm,

showing it to him. Bayir explained to Volodya how the *ongon* would come. At first the spirit would descend to the *Serge* and travel through all the trees that were united by the red thread. Then he would come to Volodya through the *Ur* Tree under which the meat offering stood. Volodya started chanting again but could not remember the words and did not fall into a rhythm. The rhythm of the chant is very important. Every shaman must find his own beat from within. The rhythm of the chant must pulse within him like his heart. But the sense of his own heartbeat seemed to escape Volodya.

Bayir decided to help Volodya and called for his own drum and headdress. He sat on a stool behind Volodya and started

chanting. He hoped this would help push Volodya into a rhythm. Indeed, Volodya started to drum, but he failed to find a steady beat. When Bayir built to climax, Volodya did not and Bayir pulled off his headdress.

Bayir, however, was not willing to give up yet. He had the Children of Heaven continue to chant as the assistants brought Volodya's *arkhali*. This is a special part of the ritual outfit that is worn on the shoulders and back. It consists of a metal frame that has a large piece of brocade sewn onto it that forms a narrow cape on the shaman's back. In front the metal frame supports the heads of two large vipers made of black velvet that stand on both sides of the shaman's face. Their tails, as well as numerous smaller snakes,

flow down the shaman's back. Both of Volodya's ancestors had apparently requested that such an *arkhali* be made. As the shamans tried to dress Volodya, Bayir noticed that the *arkhali* was not sewn right. He asked for a knife and with Bolod-Akhe's help he redid the way it tied. Volodya was dressed again in his feathered *orgay* and readied for the next ritual.

Bayir explained to Volodya that during the *Tohorulkha* or Bring up the Dust Ritual he must run around the birches of the northern grove, having lost all sense of himself. His own ancestors should push him, propel him, to climb one of the two trees at the north end of the grove. These were the Mother and Father Trees. If Volodya climbed the Father Tree it would be with the help of Zandan Babey and then he should make offerings only to the ancestor spirits of his father's line. If he climbed the Mother Tree it would be with Buzhagar Babey's help and then Volodya should make offerings to his ancestors on his grandfather's mother's side. Bayir also told Volodya that he would be allowed to rest after nine rounds around the grove. Each *Tohorulkha* Ritual would consist of three sets of nine rounds. Then Bayir told the assistants to be on guard since Volodya could run every which way.

Volodya stood and started trotting around the birches, hitting the drum occasionally. The Children of Heaven followed. After each set of nine rounds, he rested. Volodya seemed to be making an honest effort, but after each try he was only physically exhausted. It was clear that no spirits were helping him. This *Tohorulkha* should have been with Buzhagar Babey's help, which should have propelled him up the Mother Tree. But the ancestor to whom Volodya had always prayed did not seem to be with him now.

There was one moment when Volodya started to run, but Bato-Bolot lunged after him and caught Volodya. Seseg immediately sensed that Bato-Bolot made a mistake. "Why did you stop him?" she yelled. Bayir also felt Volodya was stopped too early. To give Volodya an extra boost, Bayir took a swig of vodka and sent a spray of alcohol in Volodya's face. Then he sent Volodya off to try again. But this was a wild attempt, with no focus.

After a short break Dulma started to chant in the southern edge of the northern grove, while Bayir chanted from the northern edge. Volodya sat in front of Bayir. They chanted to the local spirits and Volodya's ancestors asking for their help. Volodya was again dressed in shaman horns. As Volodya stood up and started around the birch trees, Dulma ran and drummed alongside, trying to help him. Later Bato-Bolot and Seseg also ran alongside Volodya

Father of the Ritual smokes on a break

Olya holds the orgay

trying to help. But Volodya only walked around ponderously and the Children followed listlessly. One birch branch constantly got tangled on Volodya's fancy shaman's horns.

After a few rounds all the participants were obviously tired and Volodya did some truly uninspired slow rounds. These angered Dulma. "What are you doing?" she shouted. "Do you think you're out here for a stroll? Chant! Pray! We're all working like idiots and you are gallivanting out here!"

It was time for a break. The Children of Heaven all ran off together. The shamans smoked. Olya examined Volodya's ritual objects, as Tuyana explained the various parts. For Volodya's second attempt at *Tohorulkha* Bayir suddenly said, "Let's call Zandan Babey." This was Volodya's ancestor who'd been called down that morning and had said he'd step aside. But the results were no different. Bayir asked Volodya, "Did someone come?" "No," replied Volodya. When Bayir asked, "What are you seeing? Are you ready?" Volodya didn't answer.

Bayir decided that it was time for a longer break. During one of the meals Sayan had showed the shamans various types of throat singing. This is a traditional vocal technique that allows one person to make two sounds simultaneously. One sound is a low rumbling drone, while the other is a high-pitched whistle that carries the melody. Long ago shamans used throat singing at their rituals. They also played traditional instruments such as the metal jaw harp and the *morin khur*, or horse-head fiddle, which is a bowed two-stringed instrument that can sound like a cello.

The Children of Heaven had heard about Sayan's throat singing demonstration and now asked that he teach them how to do it. Sayan laughed and told them that it takes a lot of practice to produce even the simplest version of this difficult technique. He offered to teach them a song and told them that several years ago at a shaman ritual he had attended one of the spirits had asked the participants to sing a *Neryelge*, an ancient Thunder Dance song. No one present knew what that was, so instead they sang a contemporary Buryat romance. Their song didn't really satisfy the spirit. Shortly afterwards Sayan learned a *Neryelge* from an old woman in Tsagaan Chelutay. Long ago she had been one of the Children of Heaven at a shaman ritual. Then he learned a few more Thunder Songs and decided to include them in a theater piece he was

Sayan teaches the children a Neryelge, *or Thunder Dance Song*

creating with Yara Arts Group. The Thunder Dance songs formed one of the central scenes in the show. The Children, of course, said they wanted to learn a song like that. They sat in a half-circle and learned the words and melody.

> Are those swans flying high in the sky?
> I sing ho-hey
> Do they gaze from above on our land?
> I sing ho-hey
> Is that new way coming to our land?
> I sing ho-hey
> Will this way bring good times to us all?
> I sing ho-hey
>
> Are those hawks flying high in the sky?
> I sing ho-hey
> Do they gaze from above on our waters?
> I sing ho-hey
> Does the khan send his men to our land now?
> I sing ho-hey
> Will our people take them as their own?
> I sing ho-hey

Are those vultures flying high in the
    sky?
I sing ho-hey
Do they gaze from above on our
    herds?
I sing ho-hey
Are those hangmen I see coming to
    our land?
I sing ho-hey
As they ride does death ride through
    our land?
I sing ho-hey

The Children were told the story of Balzhan Khatan, a twenty-year-old Buryat princess who led her people out of Manchuria into the Aga steppe. The Thunder Dance the Children learned obliquely referred to the story of her journey. A large army led by a Manchurian Khan pursued her throughout the steppe. She finally surrendered in 1604 on the condition that her people be left unharmed and allowed to stay in this region. She sealed the agreement with her head, and the Buryats did not forget her sacrifice. The names of the hills, rivers, and settlements of the area tell the story of her journey. There is Togoota, where she left her *togoo* or kettle, Altan Emelte, where she left her "golden saddle," Udaganta, where she left her *udagan* or shamaness, and Ingede, the river where she surrendered by saying *"Ingede"* or "I am here."

The Children learned quickly. The Thunder Dance song started to resonate through the sacred grounds. But then the Children were called back to the northern grove where Volodya again chanted to his ancestors. Bayir sat behind Volodya trying to help. Dulma ran alongside drumming. Bayir tried to pick up the rhythm, but Volodya did not follow. After two sets of nine times around the birches all the participants looked beat.

The shamans then decided to try to Bring up the Dust on the White side. On the White side there were no trees that Volodya would have to climb. Here he would have to "lose" himself in a running ecstasy. Volodya was dressed in his White headdress and shaman's cape and given his dragon staff and bell. Seseg sat down behind him. She called to Buzhagar Babey, Volodya's ancestor.

Head thrown back, Seseg seemed to reach for inspiration. By contrast Volodya sat ringing his bell out of rhythm and twisting his staff into the ground. Seseg traced a circle at the center of Volodya's back with her bell as if to push her own energy into him. But Volodya simply stood and paraded around the trees, with no sense of the pulsing bell. The Children followed spiritlessly. Seseg raised her *bardag*, slowly waved it a few times, and then let her hand drop.

Bolod-Akhe helps Seseg-Abgey with her headdress as she prepares to chant behind Volodya on the White side

During the final set Seseg ran alongside Volodya, ringing her bell in his ear. But Volodya only seemed dazed. The shamans conferred briefly and started to leave. Seseg sat alone, looking at the birches. Then she slowly got up and followed the dispersing crowd. As Bayir had said before the first *ongon* had even descended, the shamans could not make Volodya do anything. They could only listen to what his ancestors said. Volodya's ancestors were painfully silent now.

Everyone was tired and confused by the events of the day. As the Yara team sat down to review what we were documenting, we started to argue. I stormed off and, of course, couldn't fall asleep for a long time. Then in the middle of the night someone woke me up. Bayir had decided the time had come to have Volodya try to call to his ancestors again and wanted all of us present. By the time I got dressed, all the participants were lined up in their familiar positions and Volodya was walking around the birch trees in the dark. But the results were no different than they had been during the day.

Bayir then called down Khukheron Boo. This *ongon*, as Bayir had told us, arrived with a lot of noise and anger. In the middle of her dialogue with the spirit, Dulma-Abgey yelled out, "Sayan, come here." The *ongon* was inquiring about the outsiders who were part of the ritual. I became very concerned. Perhaps we were going to be asked to leave.

Sayan ran over to the *ongon* and knelt and bowed, putting his head under the spirit's drum. Khukheron Boo asked, "Where are you from?" Sayan said he was from the Khurge-Khalbin clan and recited his ancestor line: "Borse-Dakhaley-Damdin-Zhambal-Tsedyp-Sayan." The spirit was familiar with the family. He was the grandson of Morkho-Tsedyp, who is the master of the sacred place in Argali where Sayan's family makes offerings. The spirit reminded everyone of his fate:

> I was executed
> In 1929
> In a faraway northwest land
> During hard times.

But then he blessed Sayan:

> May your son
> Have a son.
> May your daughter
> Have a daughter.
> What I did not have time to experience,
> May you experience.
> What joy I did not feel, may you feel.
> Walk through the entire world
> And see what I did not see.
> When hard times come,

Look towards Aga
And cry: "Tsydenzhab, Lord help me!"
And I will help you.
I have protected your clan for seventy years
From the bald man.
And now I give you my protection
For the next seventy years.

The *ongon* then asked Sayan what he did. Sayan answered
that he sang songs and made shows. The *ongon* yelled out, "You
sing songs and make shows? Do you know a *Neryelge*?" Sayan
answered that he knew several Thunder Dance songs, and his
voice filled the dark of the night:

Till the sun sets beyond low hills
We will thunder, we will dance!
We'll bring to life the ancient ways
Of our forefathers as we dance!

The harsh tone in Khukheron Boo's voice softened and he even
hummed along. "It's been seventy years since I heard this Thunder
Dance song. Now my soul has melted. It has melted to the core,"
said Khukheron Boo. Then he wanted to know about the other
outsider. I was called and knelt in front of the *ongon*, placing my
head under his drum. He hit it and the sound resonated inside my
head, which suddenly felt as large as a cavern. Dulma said
something to introduce me. Then the spirit said:

May you live ninety-nine years.
I will be your protector.
When hard times come
You should remember to cry:
"Tsydenzhab, Lord help me!"
And I will help you.

Then Kukheron Boo hit me hard with his *bardag* to confirm
his blessing. Someone helped me up and I started back to my place
in the dark. I stumbled on some uneven ground, but someone else's

arm steadied me and pulled me into the circle of shaman assistants. Even in the dark I could see they were all smiles. Someone whispered how wonderful it must be to have such a great protector. After that night the circle always welcomed me as one of its own. But now I was exhausted. Although the ritual was obviously not over I crawled off to sleep.

Dulma, as the khelemershen, *speaks to the* ongon *sitting in the birch grove near the meat offering*

A Cold Wind Blows

It was very cold the next morning. The wind blew right through my bones, reminding me this was Siberia. I put on all the clothes I had in my bag, layering clean t-shirts on top of dirty ones, sweaters on top of vests. Then I put on the down coat Sayan's mother had lent me. So far, I had been using it as a sleeping bag. I walked over to the place where we washed. I let the water drip on my fingertips. It was freezing cold. I dabbed my eyelids and considered myself "washed."

At breakfast I learned that events the previous night had taken a darker turn after I left. Tuyana had started chanting to her *ongon*, Ashata. When the spirit descended into her he was very, very angry. He did not say much, but he ran around, lashing out at people with his *bardag* and yelling.

Later, I learned why Tuyana's ancestor was so mad. Shaman rituals usually begin in May when the first leaves appear on the birches in the area. At this time the shamans of Bayir's circle all gather and do a ritual that will give them strength to conduct the rituals they will have to perform during the season that ends when the leaves fall in the autumn. Shortly after the May opening, Volodya had invited Tuyana to do a ritual with him. One of his brothers wanted a special cleansing. Volodya had previously told Bayir that his brother wanted a cleansing ritual. Bayir said he'd do it later because he was busy and left. Volodya then decided to do the ritual on his own and he let Tuyana believe that Bayir had approved this. Volodya had also made a mistake during this ritual. He did not raise a *hadak*, or ritual cloth, to his *bardag*. Tuyana's ancestor believed that as a result of this mistake Tuyana had cut her hand and her family's blood had been spilt. Ashata Bural Babey blamed Volodya for this. He was especially offended that Volodya had deceived Tuyana. Now Tuyana's spirit was taking his revenge on Volodya. He had closed Volodya's road and taken part of the *Shanar's* meat offering. After Ashata Bural Babey's spirit left Tuyana, the shamans conferred about the latest revelations long into the night.

Bayir decorates the Zalma *Tree offered to Tuyana's ancestor*

BELOW: *Lida, Volodya's wife, with a* hadak

OPPOSITE: *Volodya carries the* Zalma *Tree. Dulma chants below.*

The spirit of Ashata had to be appeased before the ritual could continue. The next morning, Bayir had a special *Zalma* or Offering Tree made to be raised to Tuyana's ancestor. A birch tree was brought into the *ger* and Bayir chanted to "give breath" to it. Then it was decorated with the same type of power flags that had been used to decorate the Black *Zalma* Tree outside. As Bayir chanted, Dulma held the power flags over the sacred smoke and "fed" them milk. Bayir tied the flags of the sun, moon, and various animals, according to the Black order. He explained that the number of fringes on each power flag depended on the number of *Shanars* the dedicating shaman had. Here the number referred to Volodya's *Shanars*, not Bayir's. Volodya stood and watched as Bayir wound the red thread on the birch and inserted the red arrowheads into the trunk of the tree.

Bayir then told Volodya to take the tree and go with Tuyana to the place where she made her offerings. They were to go up the hill without going to the very top, because that would be presumptuous. There they were to put the tree into the ground, making sure that the four arrowheads lined up with the Four Directions. They were then to take several steps down toward the west, make a fire, and sprinkle their offerings. "Burn what needs to be burned," Bayir said. "Sit there for five minutes and see what happens. Don't say anything unnecessary. Then you can return."

Voloyda's wife, Lida, came into the *ger* with a blue *hadak*. She had obviously been crying. Volodya picked up the tree and carried it out. He walked with it around the *ger* several times. Then he climbed up into the back of a pickup truck, still holding the tree. Tuyana got in and they drove off. Bayir turned to all the participants and said, "We will wait till they get back."

When Volodya and Tuyana returned, Dulma sat in front of the northern grove of birches and started her chant to give power to her ritual objects. She then called to her own ancestors to give her the strength to give Volodya a push. She chanted for a very long time. The group behind her seemed more tense than usual. Then she raised the fringe on her headdress and asked for a cup of tea. Bayir asked her, "How is it?" Dulma was silent for a long, long time. Then shook her head. A hush descended on all the participants.

Although it was August, the cold wind blew right through my winter jacket and all the layers I had managed to squeeze on underneath it. I decided to warm up near the kitchen fire. I listened to the women chat as they prepared our meal. They were all related to Volodya and were now very concerned about the ritual. Several wondered about Volodya's behavior. I mentioned that I noticed that the leader of the Children of Heaven was very attentive and watched all the proceedings carefully. The ladies told me he was called Zodbo and was Volodya's oldest son. They confided that they believed the shamans had lost contact with the spirits. If this was true and Voloyda failed to complete the ritual, there could be terrible implications for his family. His children could be in a life-threatening situation.

The shamans decided to have Volodya try the Bring up the Dust Ritual again. This time Volodya was dressed in Bayir's *orgay*. Perhaps his teacher's shaman's horns would help propel him. Dulma chanted

behind Volodya's back. Seseg walked alongside Volodya for a set and then Dulma ran with him. Soon they were passing him between themselves like a baton in a relay race. Again a birch branch kept getting in Volodya's way. The other participants were giving it their all, but Volodya was "just walking around with his mouth open," as Dulma put it. "Come on, big guy, take bigger steps," Seseg yelled. The assistants tried to inspire Volodya by letting out yelps as he passed by. Everyone was really hoping that each round would be the one that sent Volodya running, inspired by his spirits. The difficult situation was bringing us together. The documentary team members were now active participants. Professor Margarita let out whoops with the assistants, Sayan started running

with the shamans, and I could be heard humming the refrain. Then Bato-Bolot tried to get Volodya going, but with no results. Volodya was allowed to rest. As the shamans started to undress Volodya from Bayir's *orgay*, he chuckled. Seseg hissed, "Don't you dare laugh."

Then Bayir put on his own *orgay* and chanted to Buzhagar Babey. Tuyana and Volodya sat next to each other on the bench behind Bayir, but Tuyana turned sharply away from her colleague. The *ongon* descended and Dulma offered him yellow-red tea. Tuyana and Volodya both approached the spirit to beg for forgiveness. Tuyana expressed her deepest regrets, but Volodya was tongue-tied. Tuyana kept on prodding Volodya speak to the spirit and ask for forgiveness. Seseg whispered to him, trying to help him find the right words. They offered the *ongon* a pipe. The spirit threw it away without a word. The message was clear enough.

After the *ongon* left Bayir, his fingers and hands started cramping. He looked exhausted. His face had the same ashen color as one of my friends before he had a heart attack. I was afraid for Bayir's health. I was also afraid that if we lost him, we would lose hold of the fragile thread that linked these people to their

OPPOSITE, ABOVE: *Bayir chants in shaman's horns*

OPPOSITE, BELOW: *An* ongon *sits on an* olbok

ABOVE: *Volodya rubs Bayir's back after the spirit has left him*

traditions. The other shamans rushed to Bayir. Bato-Bolot helped undress him, and Seseg massaged his hands.

After a break, Bayir looked much better. He chanted for a very long time. Perhaps he was asking forgiveness for overestimating the strength of his student. Then Volodya was dressed in Bayir's *orgay* again. He sat still as Bayir again sprayed him with vodka from each of the Four Directions. Then Bayir also sprayed the soles of Volodya's feet. Bayir sat down in back of Volodya and started to chant. Volodya stood and started on the sixteenth set of nine rounds around the birch trees. He ran one round, instilling some hope, and then another, but soon his momentum dissipated and he started trotting around with little heart, the Children in tow. Bato-Bolot tried to help by running alongside, and Dulma and Seseg joined in, again passing Volodya between them. Bayir continued to chant even during the break. Dulma ran alongside Volodya for the final rounds. The Children were clearly tired. A break was called.

During the break Volodya sat alone as a big conference of shamans took place behind him. Eventually, Bayir asked Volodya

to join them. "Volodya, what are we going to do?" he asked. But Volodya said little. The Father and Mother of the ritual joined the circle, as did Lida, Volodya's wife. Volodya held his head in his hands. The shamans smoked. The conference continued for a long, long time, despite the numbing cold.

Eventually, some people moved inside the *ger*. It was warm inside, but the atmosphere was thicker than the black smoke bellowing out from under the damp firewood. Tuyana was sitting in the northwest section, chanting on the Black side. She beat her drum in a nervous, unsteady rhythm. Soon she was also crying. As tears ran down her face and the black fringe stuck to her cheeks, she continued to call to Volodya's ancestor Buzhagar Babey, asking for help. She paused to sprinkle her shaman's whip with vodka. She also dipped her *toibur* or shaman's drumstick into the vodka. Then she told the Guardian of the Ritual to sprinkle the vodka outdoors in the northwest direction and he did so.

Tuyana launched into another chant. I watched her beat her drum very quickly and noticed that she was firmly holding her drum. Her hand was clearly healing. Volodya came in and sat down next to her. Tuyana called to Ashata Bural Babey, her own *ongon*. She repeated Volodya's information to the spirit: "He is forty-seven, born the Year of the Horse, son of Zhalsab. He raised this *Shanar*." Volodya sat holding his head in his hands. Tuyana paused to wipe her face. Olya brought her some tea, which she sipped. Then Tuyana put her headdress back on and continued her chant. The Children of Heaven sensed that they should help her and started singing the Black refrain with her. But Volodya just lit a cigarette. Tuyana turned to Volodya and asked him the name of his clan. He answered, "Modon Khargana," and yawned. Tuyana continued to chant, but the smoky warmth inside eventually started to affect everyone. Several of the Children of Heaven were visibly falling asleep.

The atmosphere changed immediately when Bayir and the other shamans entered the tent. The Children sat right up. One of the boys complained that there was a swelling on his arm. Bayir looked at it and said, "A bee probably stung you, or maybe a mosquito. Or perhaps one of the girls pinched you." Everyone laughed.

Bayir sat down in the northwest part of the *ger* and said that we should know some things about Volodya's ancestors and family history. Sayan asked if there had been other *Shanars* like this before. Bayir said, "Yes, there have been other difficult *Shanars* like this. If Harme Zarin said, 'There is much to grasp,' it means that we will have problems and will have to understand them before we can solve them. This guarantees that the ritual will last at least three days and will not be easy.

"If we don't finish this ritual then the eleven families of this clan will start to die out. This can take ninety-nine years. The eldest son is here, so are other relatives, and they are not at fault. The spirit who was protecting them for many years, Buzhagar Babey, is very offended that he was not taken into consideration. Because of this he has closed the road. 'Since I'm not your direct relative,' he said, 'I can leave.' Now everything is suspended between heaven and earth. An offering takes only thirty minutes. It is not a difficult thing to do. But those thirty minutes in the future, in the ninth generation, in ninety-nine years, can have huge repercussions. An entire family can be wiped off the face of the earth. Because of this, we should not worry about spending a week here, so that this clan can enjoy happiness for ninety-nine years. One of Volodya's sons is among the Children of Heaven. He is not at fault here.

Zodbo, Volodya's eldest son and the leader of the Children of Heaven

"The fault lies long, long ago. Somewhere far in the north someone in Volodya's clan killed a shamaness and her daughter. Then people started dying, the clan was disappearing. In the dark of night two people were called and told to go far away. They came to Khulinda; now it's called The Victory Collective Farm. There one of them married and had a son and daughter. After that he decided to become a *lama*, a monk at the Buddhist temple. He thought: 'When I become a *lama*, I will be able to protect my children.' Some time later another man married his wife and moved with her two children here to Chelutay. The children started to get very sick. The new husband saw that there was a *dakhul*, or mark, on the children. So, he called Regsel Boo, a shaman who lived in the village who was very strong. Regsel Boo chanted and learned the whole story of the family. He then awoke the spirit of Buzhagar Babey and had him place a protection on the children. During World War II Regsel Boo and the man were called off to war. Before leaving, Regsel Boo told the man's wife, 'Don't worry, your husband will return. But I will not.' He did a ritual for the children and left. And indeed the husband returned, but the shaman did not. After the war the couple had two more children, Volodya and his twin sister Sonya. Volodya was chosen to continue the shaman line. You understand?" Bayir asked Sayan. "Yes. But it is complicated." Bayir laughed. "When two sides of one clan ordered the same unusual ritual object[1] I immediately suspected that there would be a problem, that a tug-of-war might arise. Complicated, isn't it, Sayan?" Sayan answered, "Yes. Yesterday someone said, 'It's better to know nothing, than to know this.'" "You mean it is easier to sing songs, isn't it?" Bayir laughed. "Yes, exactly," answered Sayan. "On the other hand," Bayir said, "this can be a learning experience for you."

Bayir then prepared to call down Harme Zarin, the old man who had always given him such good advice. As Volodya sat next to him, Bayir chanted inside the *ger*. Then the *ongon* of Harme Zarin entered him.

DULMA: Babey, please sit on the *olbok*. We have placed the traditional pillow right behind you. (The *ongon* was breathing heavily.) Babey, please have some of our yellow-red tea.

(HARME asked her something but it was inaudible.)

DULMA: Babey, a few days and a few nights. The young man from the Modon Khargana clan is called Volodya and is forty-seven years old. He was born in the Year of the Horse. He can't seem to complete this matter.[2] He is a late, dear son.

(HARME said something and again it was inaudible.)

DULMA: Yes, there is much to grasp. We are trying to grasp all of it. It is very difficult to complete this beautiful golden *Shanar*. There is a tug-of-war going on. Our *Shanar* has been stolen.

HARME: (inaudible)

DULMA: Yes. Yes. This late, dear son made a mistake. He took the girl who is from beautiful Chelutay, of the Bataney clan, called Tuyana, to a certain event. He did not raise a blue *hadak* at this event, and because of this she cut her hand and spilled blood. Now her ancestor, Ashata, is very offended and stands in the way of our matter. He says he stole our *Shanar* and we don't know what to do.

[1] The unusual ritual object was the *arkhali*, the cape with serpents described on page 121.
[2] The shamans and spirits sometimes do not refer to a ritual directly by name, but instead call it "this matter" or "this event."

(HARME was breathing heavily and asked a question.)

DULMA: Yes, we listened to them. We did exactly what they told us. Tuyana and Volodya took the *Zalma* Tree with all of the proper decorations and offerings to Tuyana's sacred place.

(HARME asked something.)

DULMA: We listened to what Buzhagar Babey said.

(HARME asked something.)

DULMA: The *ongon* who descended with the large shaman's horns left offended at these children. "You do not consider me a direct relative. I guess you don't need me anymore." This is what he said and then he left. It is a difficult situation; we cannot leave these children in this situation.

(HARME said something Dulma did not understand and the *ongon* repeated the question.)

DULMA: Yes, he took a wife with two children.

(HARME was breathing heavily and said something.)

DULMA: Yes. Yes. We listened to what he said. When he left offended, we did what he wanted.

(HARME asked something.)

DULMA: A trough?

(HARME asked again. Dulma did not understand. The *ongon* repeated the question.)

DULMA: This is the best meat. It is the *tole*.[3]

(Someone approached Dulma and whispered in her ear.)

DULMA: The right side of the meat with the shoulder blade is missing. But the soup from that meat is here.

(HARME asked something.)

DULMA: Who is higher? Shatey Babey is higher.[4]

(HARME said something.)

DULMA: Please repeat that.

(HARME repeated what he said.)

DULMA: The girl's bones were not broken. She only spilled a little blood. He was offended because there was deception and they did not raise a *hadak*.

(HARME said something.)

DULMA: Our Wagon Master? (This is what the *ongons* called Bayir.) No, he is not offended.[5] He is trying to make the situation better.

(HARME said something inaudible and ended with): Listen to the high *ongons* of this land.

DULMA: Yes, Babey. Do you think the two great *ongons*, who are offended at these two late children, will cause problems for the next generation?

HARME: Do you have a spear?

DULMA: Well, there is a little one on my robe.[6]

HARME: Well, just use your spear to separate them. Now, give me a hand.

DULMA: Babey, please help these late children from your side.

The spirit jumped, round and round, and left Bayir. This raised a great cloud of dust. Dulma yelled for the Cupbearers to bring water and sprinkle it on the ground. Seseg wiped Bayir's face and massaged his hands. Dulma brought him tea. Then the shamans conferred about the meaning of Harme's statements.

---

[3] When the sheep is slaughtered in a traditional manner, the head, esophagus, and all the organs are left attached in one piece. This is called the *tole* and is usually the main part of an offering.

[4] Here "higher" means further up the ancestor line. Shatey Babey was the father of Buzhagar Babey.

[5] Interesting moment when the *ongon* thinks that perhaps Bayir is offended and this is the problem.

[6] Shamans have tiny metal weapons decorating their robes.

Dulma reported, "Harme told us how to rearrange the meat offering. He also said, 'Call down Buzhagar Babey and his father,
Shatey Babey. Listen to what he has to say.'" Harme was advising
the shamans to turn to the father of Buzhagar Babey for help in
separating the two warring shamans. "Harme said," Dulma continued, "the two great *ongons* must be led in separate directions. If

the situation becomes really difficult, call down the Manzhiley, Master of the *Shanar*. He has the right to accept any *Shanar*."

Bayir asked for a cigarette. Dulma handed him one and he lit it. Dulma continued, "Harme said, 'Tuyana's ancestor didn't lose any children. I don't see the reason why he is so offended.'" Bayir decided to take Harme's advice and call Shatey Babey. Dulma added, "You know, Harme asked me if I had a spear. When I said I had a little one on my robe, he said, 'Why are you afraid of them, just stick them with it.'" Everyone laughed because the spear Dulma had on her robe was tiny, only about an inch or two long. Dulma then said to Bayir, "He also asked about you. 'Your Wagon

Master is not offended, is he?' Then the spirit said, 'If he was offended, you would tell this insane old man, wouldn't you?'" Everyone laughed. The *ongon* was speaking about Bayir through Bayir's body.

The shamans and all the other participants walked out of the *ger* and gathered at the northern grove. Bayir prepared to chant to Shatey Babey, father of Buzhagar Babey. The Guardian of the Ritual ran around the offering with the sacred smoke. Bayir put on his shaman's horns as the Children chanted in the background. Bayir sat down to chant and soon the *ongon* entered him. He walked all bent up into the birch grove. The Children covered their eyes, not only out of reverence for the spirit, but also because the wind was blowing mercilessly. The *ongon* was silent for a long time. Then Volodya was summoned. He bowed in front of the spirit. The *ongon* examined Voldoya's ritual objects. Dulma offered the spirit vodka. He took it, blessed it, and had Volodya sprinkle it. The second time Dulma offered the spirit vodka, he drank it. The

ongon stood up and the Children cowered. Then he shook and jumped and left Bayir. Bayir again looked exhausted and recovered very slowly.

The weather was worsening. It was very cold and windy when Bayir sat down behind Volodya and started chanting. Volodya got up and started running. But he ran wildly, heading for the women who gathered to watch. The assistants caught him before anyone was hurt. I noticed that one of the elderly women wore dark sunglasses even though the sky was covered with clouds. It was the grandmother who had cut her forehead on the *ongon's* shaman's horns two days earlier. Perhaps she had put on the glasses so that the spirits would not recognize her now.

The assistants undressed Volodya and let him rest. He ran again in the next set, but this time he slipped and fell. Someone told him to change his shoes. His son, who led the Children of Heaven, took off his Adidas sneakers and offered them to his dad. But the assistants didn't give Volodya the time to change his shoes and rushed him off to do another round. Soon it became apparent that nothing much would happen and they undressed Volodya. Bayir told the assistants that the northern grove had to be repaired. All the broken birch branches had to be anointed with butter.

After the repairs were done, Bayir chanted without putting on his shaman's horns. The *ongon* of Buzhagar Babey entered him. The spirit was silent for a long time, and then he summoned Volodya who knelt and bowed before the spirit. Bato-Bolot lit a pipe to have it ready just in case the spirit requested it. The last time this spirit came he refused the pipe and threw it to the ground. Perhaps now he would accept it. Everyone huddled against the cold wind, tense, unable to look away, afraid they might miss something important. Tuyana crouched down near Volodya's wife as the spirit touched Volodya's head.

DULMA: These late children were told to make offerings to both their ancestors and to the Master of Red Mountain. We were told to make all these offerings, Buzhagar Babey.

BUZHAGAR: (said something but the wind blew so strongly that nothing was heard although the spirit spoke for a long time.)

DULMA: I don't understand you, Babey.

(BUZHAGAR said something.)

DULMA: Where is the *bardag*? (Someone brought Volodya's shaman's whip.) Here it is.

(BUZHAGAR lifted the *bardag* and said something.)

DULMA: Yes. Yes. Yes.

A strong gust of wind blew again and the leaves rustled, as the *ongon* left Bayir. The shamans gathered inside the *ger* for a conference. Dulma told the others that the spirit had said, "I will make him run up the birch. I thought you raised the *Shanar* to Manzhiley and therefore I did not come. I am glad that you called me now and made offerings to me before raising the *Shanar*. I will make Volodya run up the Mother's Tree. Don't let him climb too high. Take him down immediately. When he grabs the tree with his hands, the power will enter his fingers. I will forgive the spirit who tried to spoil my *Shanar*. Or I will spoil his attempt." At first Buzhagar was somewhat angry, Dulma told them, but then he told Tuyana and Volodya that he would help and protect them. He told Volodya, "Look after and protect your clan. Be braver with people. In times of trouble cry 'Eagle Buzhagar Babey' and I will come and help you."

Bayir asked what the spirit did when he was angry. Dulma said he kept hitting things with his *bardag*. Then he drank tea while she talked and talked. This seemed to calm him down, she said. "So, we should push on," Bayir said.

Bringing up the Dust

Everyone gathered outside at the northern grove. I noticed that during the break Volodya had put on his son's sneakers. We all watched as Volodya was dressed in his cape of snakes and shaman's horns. The *ongon* had said Volodya would now run. Everything had to be done just right. As we all concentrated on Volodya and the preparations I saw Bayir walk away. Perhaps he was too concerned to watch, perhaps he felt too responsible for his student.

Bayir knew how hard the next part would be for Volodya. "During my first *Shanar*," Bayir had told me, "I became very frightened and thought I was dying. I had the feeling that my soul flew

Bringing up the Dust on the Black side

Bringing up the Dust on the White side

out. I saw the whole region, the whole local area below me as if I was flying in a very fast plane. When I came to, everyone was crying. I've had three *Shanars* now. During each *Shanar* I ran up the Father Tree. My robes and instruments themselves weigh over sixty kilos, yet I become weightless in those moments."

Now, as Volodya got up and started around the birches, everyone began to yell, "Go! Go! Go! Forward!" Even Professor Margarita was jumping up and down. "Let him run! Let him run!" she yelled. Volodya started running, but then he slipped and fell. The assistants rushed to pick him up and set him running without a break. On his next attempt, it happened. Everything suddenly came together. Volodya ran around the birches and the Children dashed in back of him, barely keeping up. Something was clearly pushing Volodya beyond himself. Volodya let go of his drum and suddenly climbed up the Mother Tree. We all held our breath. The assistant rushed to pull him down. They grabbed Volodya before he managed to get too high up the tree, just as the spirits had suggested.

After they pulled him down, Volodya was sick to his stomach and breathing heavily. Tears ran down his face. Seseg hit him with the *bardag* on his back and chest. She gave him some tea and massaged his hands. Then she took a swig from the bottle of vodka and sprayed Volodya's face with vodka.

The shamans immediately moved to the southern birch grove, and readied to have Volodya Bring up the Dust on the White side. The Children started chanting, *"Padme hum om mani."* Seseg sat down behind Volodya and started to chant before Volodya was even dressed. Volodya was given his cape, dragon staff, and bell. Seseg paused as Volodya turned to her and asked her something several times. Seseg started to chant again and Volodya almost fell into the rhythm of her chant. Seseg blessed him with her *bardag* and again reached for inspiration as she threw her head back, chanting. Suddenly, Volodya stood up and started running. Bato-Bolot and the Leader of the Children ran desperately behind him and finally helped catch him. Seseg ran up to the crowd that was barely restraining the "tall pale man." She rang the bell and hit Volodya with a *bardag* on his back, chest, and legs.

The shamans decided that Volodya's first run was with Buzhagar Babey's help. This meant that his ancestor to whom he had always prayed helped him both climb the Mother Tree and Bring up the Dust on the White side.

Seseg decided to have Volodya try to Bring up the Dust with the help of his other ancestor. She again sat down behind Volodya, who was already ringing his bell and chanting. Volodya turned to her and asked her to sit closer to him. Seseg moved up her stool and started to chant. To everyone's surprise now we clearly heard Volodya chanting out loud with Seseg. Volodya was now also keeping Seseg's rhythm. Seseg stood and Volodya got up to run around the birches. The Children took off after him. Bato-Bolot again gave chase, and, with the other male assistants, caught Volodya. This second run was with the help of Zandan, Volodya's newfound relative on his father's side. Perhaps now Volodya would have the double protection that had caused him so much trouble in the past few days.

Blessings and happiness have descended!
Descended!
Joy and happiness have descended!
Descended!
May the children live beautifully forever.
The ritual is complete!
The ritual is complete!

Giving Thanks

Bayir, who was inside the *ger* when Volodya ran up the tree on the Black side and brought up the dust on the White side, came out now. He told everyone to line up to give thanks. The women from the kitchen passed out cookies and candies. We were all told to hold several of each in our hands. All the people were now invited to stand in line behind the shamans. There were so many people that three lines were formed. We stood facing west, as Seseg stood in front of us with a *hadak* spread between her hands. Bayir and Dulma joined her, also with *hadaks* stretched between their hands. The shaman assistants were in the front line holding blue *hadaks*, and next to them stood Sayan with a *hadak* I had bought a few days before in the market in Aga. Volodya stood with a pail full of the offering meat, next to his wife who held a basin. The Head of the Village Administration held the dish with the traditional white food offering. Next stood the Father, Mother, and Children of the Ritual. The line ended with the two Guardians of the Ritual and the Cupbearers. Seseg rang her bell and started to chant:

> I chant and
> Ask for blessings and happiness
> For a man called Volodya
> Who raised this yellow golden *Shanar,*

And for his wife, his faithful companion
And for his dear children
And for those who helped from their side
And for his older and younger brothers
And for his beautiful relatives
And for his beautiful friends and blood-brothers
And for the leader
Of this beautiful golden *Shanar.*

As the chant of thanks to the west ended, we all said, *"A-huray!"* We raised our palms and moved them in a circle toward the heavens. Bayir told the group to turn north. The wind stopped blowing and the sun started to break through the clouds as Seseg continued her chant:

I chant without mistake
To the beautiful North,
To the great Northern Spirits,

Khihan Ulan Tengeri,
Mother Khilma Khatan,
Darkhan Sagan Tengeri,
And Protector Damdin Dorlik.
Great Protectors
Of this land
Both near and far guardians,
The masters of *obos* and mountains,
Listen from your highest peaks.
You who dive through waters,
Listen to me, hear me well.

Then the group thanked the spirits of the east and south in a similar way. Finally, the group once again turned to all four sides and confirmed that happiness and joy had descended and that the ritual was now complete.

Bayir told everyone to sit in a circle and eat the cookies and candies they held. A light drizzle started to fall. Bayir held Volodya's *orgay* and addressed the circle: "Elder sisters and brothers, friends who helped from the side, guests, students, Father and Mother of the Ritual, Children of Heaven, Guardians of the Ritual, Cupbearers, for the last five days and nights we all made great efforts for this young man. This matter turned out to be complicated. Long, long ago somewhere in the North a great misfortune took place. People left this place and those who came here, to our land, had a protection placed on them. Then it was decided that this young man, Volodya, should continue the shaman line.

"And then a mistake occurred," Bayir continued. "Our Tuyana was not at fault. Our brother was at fault. No matter how inconvenient it is, we must tell the truth. In the future you need to find a common language, you need to understand each other better. If you do not, very bad things can take place. For five days I worked hard for this young man. And at the most important moment, my heart could not take it any more and I had to walk away. I walked away when I understood that something inside of Volodya had stirred. So, here we are. Here are the ritual objects that were ordered for him. The man who was offended had every right to feel that way. He had placed his protection on this clan, he let them multiply and become wealthy. In the future, Volodya, you must do the rituals for your brothers by yourself. You must not think that you can't. Everything will work out according to tradition. But you must remember to raise a *hadak* to your ritual objects. If you do not have a *hadak*, find a coin and place it in offering. You must believe with all your heart. Without faith nothing will take place."

Bayir continued, "We all stand together. Buryats not only from Chelutay and the eight Aga clans and the eleven Khori clans, but all Buryats on this earth will all eventually find their way to shamanism. A shaman legend tells us that there will be too many people on our earth. The planet will not be able to support this many people and there will come a time when there will be fewer people. . . . Well, I don't know if we will be alive then or not, but Tuyana, Volodya, and I will surely witness this event as *ongons*." Everyone laughed.

Bayir lifted the shaman's horns he held in his hands. "This *orgay* has now been given life and its Master is now Buzhagar Babey. Volodya has asked for blessing and happiness from the Four Directions. Let his road never be closed from all Four Directions. Let all the events he plans take place. Be brave in the events you plan, Volodya. You don't have to deceive people in this life. A man takes offense when he is beaten. A man takes offense when he is wounded with a knife. Wounds heal, but an offense caused by words can remain forever. A mistake in words is the most awful. You must remember this.

"Now," he said, "we will decorate the *orgay*. When you tie the silk and brocade, think of your own children and friends and wish them well." Dulma stepped into the circle and held the *orgay* as Bayir tied his *hadak* to Volodya's shaman's horns.

Bato-Bolot came into the circle with his *hadak*, but Bayir motioned him aside and let Seseg tie her *hadak* first to Volodya's shaman's horns. Then Tuyana tied her *hadak*, as Bato-Bolot fiddled with his belt. He was not used to letting women go first. In traditional Buryat society men always went first, but among shamans rank, not sex, determined the order. Dulma was next in line to tie her *hadak* to Volodya's *orgay*, before it was Bato-Bolot's turn. Then Bolod-Akhe stepped into the center and tied his *hadak*, as Olya waited her turn behind him. Sayan stepped up with our *hadak* and was followed by the Head Administrator of the Village. Bayir asked for scissors and cut off the long ends of all the *hadaks* that were tied to Volodya's *orgay*. He then walked up to Volodya and handed him his shaman's horns.

Seseg ties her hadak *to Volodya's* orgay

Then Bayir tied a strip of brocade to the pair of metal shaman's staves that Seseg brought into the center of the circle. He picked up the *horbo* and said, "When the *ongons* will come they will lean on these." Bayir demonstrated how the spirit will lean on the shaman staff. "Elders and youngsters, when you decorate the *horbo* with strips of brocade, think: 'May all be well with Volodya. May he live without disease and suffering.'"

Bayir then called for Volodya's *arkhali*. "This *arkhali* has twelve snakes on it. It symbolizes the Upper Heavens." He pointed to the lower part of the cape, which was made of blue brocade. "This is our blue earth. This is what is found between the two worlds," Bayir said, pointing to the upper part of the brocade. "Dulma, please take this *arkhali* and decorate it."

At that moment I looked up from the camera and noticed a rainbow. I pointed it out to Tuyana, who announced, "Look, the sun has come out, and a rainbow." People repeated, "Look, a rainbow, how beautiful." How beautiful and how perfect.

Then Sayan asked what it meant when two ends of a rainbow are in one valley. Bolod-Akhe told him he thought it meant that it will rain for a long time. Bolod-Akhe then told the crowd, "Take off your hats. This drizzle is a cleansing force. Rain that falls while there is a rainbow acquires special cleansing powers." People started taking off their hats and letting the light drizzle fall on their faces.

During the ritual I had become more and more aware of the powerful forces that surrounded us. The stars beckoned to us on clear nights. One morning thick fog clouded our vision. On another winds howled and drove huge clouds across the vast expanse of the sky, ignoring our measly petitions below. The rainbow that came out seemed to be responding to our collective joy. By coming to the ceremony we had stepped out of the daily routine of our lives and entered into a dialogue not only with each other, but with forces far beyond ourselves. The longer we stayed out there, the more we became aware of our place and the interdependence of all the elements around us. We started seeing and hearing what they had to say to us.

Seseg stepped to the center of the circle and held out the sheep kidneys. She said that this was the right kidney of the offered meat. "You should all taste how round and whole this kidney is,"

Volodya and his wife Lida try to take a bite of the khoshkhonok, *or sheep sausage*

she said. "Each one of you must taste it. You are of the Modon Khargana clan and the wives of this clan. You should be as together and whole as these round kidneys. May you become elders and live embracing your children and great-grandchildren. We who follow our protector Bayir and took part in this ritual will also taste this right kidney and wish each other well. First of all, Volodya, you should taste it." Seseg then passed the kidney around the circle according to the sun.

Then it was time to start the shaman games. Bato-Bolot stepped into the circle. He held out a sausage made of stuffed sheep intestine and said, "This is the *khoshkhonok* of our offered meat. Each one of you should taste it. Each one of you must bite off a piece without touching it with your hands. Your luck will be as big as the piece you bite off." He then walked up to Volodya and waved the intestine in front of his face. Volodya leaned forward to bite and Bato-Bolot pulled the intestines away, teasing him. Volodya missed a few more times before he managed to bite off a chunk. Bato-Bolot then moved on to the next person in the circle according to the sun. He tried to get a rise out of each person, but often Bato-Bolot himself became the butt of the joke.

Then Bayir brought out a basin full of a milky cheese. "This is the *tarag*, a very old traditional Buryat dairy product. Everyone should taste it." Bayir approached Volodya with the basin and reminded Volodya of the rules of this game, "You can't say no to any of my questions in this game." He held the basin out and asked, "Can you load seven camels?" Volodya answered yes. "Can you house nine camels?" "Yes, I can," Volodya answered and bent down to take a sip. Instead he got a face full of *tarag* as Bayir lifted the basin. Everyone howled with laughter.

Bayir then approached the next person in the circle. As soon as the person tried to take a sip, Bayir either pulled the basin away or brought it up so quickly that the person got a face full of milk. Bayir also teased each person, telling jokes and disarming the individual. Other people snuck up behind the person, ready to hold their head so they couldn't suddenly pull away from the basin.

I asked Bayir, "Why the games?" He told me that we had all worked so hard during the ritual that now we needed some laughter and joy. The shaman games were joyful and fun, until it was your turn. But even afterwards, once you wiped off the milk you soon were laughing at the attempts of others to outwit the shaman with the basin.

Bayir moved on to Oktiabrina, the Mother of the Ritual. I reminded her to take off her glasses, but she ignored me, thinking that these would somehow protect her. "Well, Mother, you now have two husbands. Will you yell at both of your husbands?" Bayir asked. "Yes, I will," she answered, remembering the rules of the

The Father of the Ritual and one of the Children of Heaven "taste" the tarag

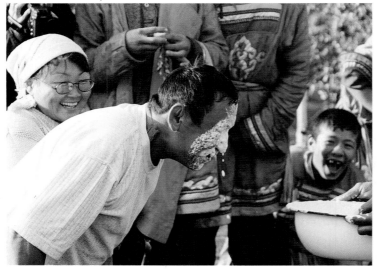

game. "Can you load seven camels?" "Yes, I can." "Will you have a child with the Father of the Ritual? Remember, you can't say no," Bayir reminded her. "What can I say? It all depends on the Father of the Ritual." Bayir turned to the circle. "People, did you hear what she said? So taste the *tarag* for your child." Bayir lifted the basin and Oktiabrina got a face full of *tarag*. Her glasses were coated with the milky cheese. She looked ready to cry, so I handed her my handkerchief. Then we both burst out laughing as the next person in line was drenched.

Bayir approached the Children of Heaven. "Can you load seven camels?" Volodya's oldest son, Zodbo, answered, "Yes, I can." "Will you marry a girl?" "Yes, I will." "Will you have children?" "Yes, I will." "Will you do good?" "Yes, I will." "For your children and for all the good you will do, taste this ritual white food from the very center of the basin." Zodbo leaned in to take a sip and Bayir raised the basin quickly. Volodya's oldest son was totally covered in milk.

Zhargal, the son of Volodya's twin sister Sonya, was next in line. Bayir held out the basin with the milky cheese in front of him and asked, "Will you live long?" "Yes, I will." "Will you have two wives?" "Yes," answered Zhargal and everyone laughed. "Is the neighbor's daughter pretty?" Bayir continued. "Yes, she is." "Will you be running to see her?" "Yes, I will," answered the boy and again everyone laughed. "So then, taste the *tarag* for the neighbor's daughter. And don't peck at it like a hen." Everyone laughed as Zhargal got a facefull of *tarag*.

Moving down the line, Bayir approached one of the girls. "Will you give birth to a boy?" he asked. "Yes, I will." "Will you get married?" "Yes, I will." "Is the neighbor's boy cute?" "Yes, he is." "Will you pay a visit this evening?" "Yes, I will," said the girl. "Listen," Bayir then said to her, "I'm not your neighbor, don't look at me like that." Everyone laughed. "So," he added in an exaggerated stage whisper, "when will you come?" and everyone laughed again.

The shamanesses were not exempt from taking a sip of *tarag*. When Bayir approached Dulma she took off her glasses and got ready. "Will you give birth to a boy?" he asked. "Yes, I will," she answered. "Who will be the father?" "Whoever," answered Dulma and the crowd laughed. "How about Sayan Zhambalov?" asked Bayir. "Where is he?" said Dulma, looking around as if she was

ready to tackle our colleague right then and there. Everyone laughed. "People, did you hear that?" announced Bayir. "Dulma said she'd have a son with Sayan Zhambalov and he will be a singer, too." Everyone laughed. Dulma then said, "I was going to dive right into the *tarag*, but I took one look and there are some hairs floating in it. Those are definitely long, female hairs. Whose are they, Bayir?" she teased and everyone laughed.

Sayan and I were not spared our turns at the basin, nor was Alexander, our photographer. I actually surprised Bayir during my turn. I carefully took off my glasses, held my hair back, and dove into the basin by myself. Volodya then held the basin for Bayir's turn. Finally, someone noticed that Seseg had managed to escape. As Seseg readied herself, Olya stepped quietly behind Seseg and held out her hand ready to catch Seseg if she tried to dodge the basin with the milky cheese. Seseg, too, was well drenched.

After the games, Bato-Bolot and the Guardians of the Ritual started to undo the red thread from the trees in the northern grove, as Dulma and the Cupbearers took apart the oil lamps. Volodya's relatives stepped up one by one and were given the meat offering, altar, and other parts that would be burned. As the northern grove was disassembled, Bayir checked in his notebook, which had a list of predictions based on how the events had proceeded. The other shamans looked on over his shoulder.

OPPOSITE: *Virlana and Shaman Bayir "taste" the* tarag

BELOW: *The women of Volodya's clan try to pull out the Mother Tree, as the men pull on the Father Tree*

Then one of the young males from Volodya's family pulled out the *Ur* Tree. As we watched, he ran with it around the *ger* several times and then headed out of the sacred grounds. He ran far off toward one of the surrounding hills in the northwest direction. There near the top he left the tree as an offering to the local Master Spirits.

A group of women from Volodya's family lined up near the Mother Tree and an equal number of males lined up near the Father Tree. Each group grabbed the trunk of their tree and tried to pull it out first. The males easily won this contest, but this was not always the case. At a ritual the next year in Romanovka we would

witness a similar contest that the women won. There the males struggled long after the females won before they finally managed to coordinate their efforts and pull out the Father Tree. At Volodya's *Shanar* the Mother Tree was stuck deep into the earth. The women managed to bend the tree to the very ground before they dislodged the buried roots. Finally, the women pulled out the Mother Tree and lined up behind the men with the Father Tree. Volodya's young relatives then pulled out the birch saplings of the northern grove one by one. They lined up behind the people holding the two larger trees. The Cupbearers and shaman assistants filled in the holes in the earth left by the trees. They poured grain and milk into the holes, begging the earth's forgiveness for the wounds they had caused. Then they covered the holes with dirt. The entire northern grove was soon undone.

Five elders from the clan stood at the north end with cups of milk. They each held a tiny branch, which they used to sprinkle the milk. Then they tossed the cups to see if the sacrifice was accepted. It was, and Bayir started to beat his drum. The people

holding the trees and offerings ran around the *ger* several times and then to the north of the sacred grounds where they stacked the trees for a bonfire. Bato-Bolot placed the altar at the center of the stacked wood and lit the fire. We watched the fire blaze and lift all the elements that had been part of the ritual to the heavens.

The participants then walked over to the southern grove, disassembled it, created a stack of wood to the south of the sacred grove and burned everything that had to be burned. Then they pulled out the trees and altars dedicated to the Four Directions and ran with them around the *ger*. They placed them on the burning bonfire in the south.

It was dark when the participants lined up on the northwest end of the sacred ground for the final chant of the ritual. Dulma beat her drum and knocked back one by one the souls of the Father, Mother, the Nine Children of Heaven, the two Guardians of the Ritual, and the two Cupbearers. The ritual was very similar to the one Bayir had performed several days earlier to knock out the

OPPOSITE: *Seseg blesses the bonfire*

ABOVE: *Dulma chants to knock back the souls of the participants*

souls of the participants to the Thirteen Northern Spirits of the Baikal. A cup of milk for each participant was placed on Dulma's drum, and the person knelt under the drum as she chanted. Then she tossed the cup. If it landed upright, they ran to it, circled it three times, picked it up, and drank whatever was left inside. Then they ran up to Tuyana who took off the red tassel, or *zala*, that had marked the fact that they were without their souls.

Bayir then spoke to the Children. "These *zala* protected you during the ritual. Now you have given them to Volodya. After this you have the right to ask him for help when you are getting married or when you are entering college. This was a difficult *Shanar*, but you should not talk badly about it. You should never pollute the water. Don't ever say this or that *ongon* was good or bad. You should hold all this inside. Someday in the future you will stand in our places. You will then remember the five days when you almost froze during Volodya's *Shanar*."

Bayir then said, "Here, Volodya, I have tied the fifteen *zala*. For the next three years during the full moon of the ninth month you must make offerings for all the participants of the ritual. So, when you grow old and wet your pants, they will come to help you step outside to piss." Everyone laughed.

It was growing cold. All the participants moved inside the *ger*. Here Volodya and his family gave presents to Bayir and all the shamans. Volodya presented Bayir with a *hadak*. Bayir pulled out a thread from it and gave the thread back to Volodya.[1] The Head Administrator of the Village received a present, as did Dulma and Seseg. According to Buryat tradition the hosts give presents to the visitors, so we too received gifts. Bayir wished Sayan a long, long life. He said about me, "I know her. I saw her home. I saw how tall the buildings are in her city. The most important thing, Virlana, is that you understand what went on here in the last four-five days and that you explain it to others."

Then Bayir asked the Children to sing the Thunder Dance Song they had learned. The Children insisted that Sayan and I help them sing. We stood together in the west end of the *ger*, where the Children had sat and slept together for five days, and sang:

---

[1] Traditionally when you receive a gift you should give something in return, even if it is only a token.

Till the sun sets beyond low hills
We will thunder, we will dance!
We'll bring to life the ancient ways
Of our forefathers as we dance!

Thanks

All the participants of the ritual deserve our deepest gratitude, especially Shaman Bayir Rinchinov, who encouraged us in our work. We would also like to thank all the Aga Buryats who shared their food, songs, and stories with us. While we waited for the ritual to begin, we stayed with Sayan's mother and brothers and we would like to thank the extended Zhambalov family for their hospitality.

Our translations from Buryat have been supported with public funds from the New York State Council on the Arts Translation Grants, as well as private funds from the Witter Bynner Foundation for Poetry Translation Award and the Nordlys Foundation, with special thanks to Barbara Glaser. We also appreciate the generous donation from Candy and David Orlinsky, who helped support this publication. In addition, we would like to thank Jim Wasserman and everyone at Parabola, especially Joe Kulin, for their work on this book.

Yara's work in Buryatia has been supported by the Trust for Mutual Understanding, Meet the Composer/International Creative Collaborations Program, in partnership with the Ford Foundation, ArtsLink, Mongol American Cultural Association, the Alliance of Resident Theaters of New York, New York Foundation for the Arts, the Edith Markson Travel Fund from Arts International, Alexandra Tkacz, and numerous friends of Yara both in New York and in Buryatia. I would like to thank Vladlen Pantaev for introducing me to our Buryat friends and Yara artists Watoku Ueno, Genji Ito, Tom Lee, Meredith Wright, Natalia Honcharenko, Cecilia Arana, Zabryna Guevara, Eleanor Lipat, Andrew Pang and Carmen Pujols for bringing so much heart to our projects in Buryatia.

Most of all, I would like to thank Ellen Stewart of La MaMa for supporting Yara's work with our Buryat colleagues. Thank you, mama, for sending me to this very special place.

— Virlana Tkacz

Glossary

Ritual objects

arkhali, shaman's cape with vipers

bardag, shaman's whip

bayag, White shaman's staff

horbo, Black shaman's staff

maykhabsha, shaman's headdress

nemerge, White shaman's cape

orgay, shaman's horns

toibur, drumstick

toli, shaman's mirror

Place names

Aga, river and regional center of the Buryat Aga Region in Eastern Siberia

Alkhanay, sacred mountain in Buryat Aga Region and nearby village

Altan Emelte, place name in Balzhan Khatan story

Argali, Sayan's family's village

Chandali, Seseg's village

Chelutay, village near the ritual site

Ingede, river's name in Balzhan Khatan story

Khulinda, Volodya's family is from this village in the North

Krasny Yar, where Khukheron Boo was shot

Kunkur, village in Buryat Aga Region

Sahanta, village where children were dying

Togoota, place name in Balzhan Khatan story

Tsagaan Chelutay, village where we learned Thunder Dance Song

Udaganta, place name in Balzhan Khatan story

People

Aryuna, Cupbearer at the ritual

Balzhan Khatan, seventeenth-century Buryat princess

Bato-Bolot, assistant White shaman

Batomunko, Father of the Ritual

Bayir Rinchinov, head shaman at the ritual

Bazar-Guro, Guardian of the Ritual on the White side

Bolod-Akhe, older assistant shaman

Chinggis Khan, or Genghis Khan as he is known in the West, was the thirteenth-century Mongol conqueror of Central Asia

Choboloy, a local shaman

Dambakha, man who slaughtered sheep

Dolgorma, Shaman Bayir's wife

Dulma Dashiyeva, Black shamaness

Head Administrator of the village

Khoridoi Mergen, the hunter who according to legend had eleven sons with the Swan Mother. The eleven Khori Buryat clans trace their origin to these sons.

Lida, Volodya's wife

Lubsan-Dagba-Akhe, Bayir's mentor in Mongolia

Oktiabrina, Mother of the Ritual

Olya, young assistant shamaness

Professor Margarita Gomboyeva, from University of Chita, a specialist in shamanism

Radna, Cupbearer at the ritual

Regsel Boo, a powerful shaman who lived in Chelutay before World War II and placed Buzhagar Babey's protection on Volodya's family

Seseg Balzhinimayeva, White shamaness, leader of the White side

Sonya, Volodya's twin sister

Tuyana, assistant Black shamaness

Volodya Zhaltsapov, dedicating shaman, for whom the *Shanar* was held

Zhalsab, Volodya's father

Zhamyan, Guardian of the Ritual on the Black side

Zhargal, Sonya's son and one of the Children of Heaven

Zodbo, Volodya's oldest son and leader of the Children of Heaven

Ongons

Ashata, Tuyana's *ongon*

Buzhagar Bural Babey, Volodya's ancestor on his grandfather's mother's
   side

Harme Zarin, spirit of old man that Bayir called

Khukheron Boo, spirit of shaman that Bayir called who was executed in
   1929

Manzhiley, Master of the *Shanar*

Shatey Babey, Buzhagar's Babey's father

Zandan Babey (or Zandan Zarin), Volodya's ancestor on his grandfather's father side

Other Terms

Abgey, term used to address respected female elders

A-huray, exclamation of affirmation

Akhe, term used to address respected male elders

Altan Serge, Golden Hitching Post Ritual, first ritual for someone stepping
   on the path to shamanism

arkhali, shaman's cape with vipers

arkhe, traditional home-brew

Aya-ganga, grass burned by Black shamans during the ritual

Babey, respectful term for father or male elder

bardag, shaman's whip

baryasha, bone-setter, a folk healer who often also serves as a midwife

Bataney, Tuyana's clan

Batey Kubdud, Bayir's clan

bayag, White shaman's staff

Bodongud, Seseg's clan

dakhul, mark

datsan, Buddhist temple

Dezhyt, spirit mistress of the area that included the sacred grounds

dudalga, words that one says to call a spirit

Ekin Khunde, Clan Ritual

Galzud, Oktiabrina's clan

ger, traditional round tent

hadak, silk ritual cloth. The preferred color is sky-blue, but *hadaks* can also be white or yellow.

horbo, Black shaman's staff

iltahan, a small piece of metal shaped like a human

khelemershen, person who speaks with the *ongon*

Khori Buryats, Eastern Buryats who trace their origin to Khoridoi Mergen, including the Buryats who live in the Buryat Aga Region

khoshkhonok, sheep sausage

Khubdud, Batamunko's clan

Khukhe Munkhe Tengeri, spirit of the Eternal Blue Heavens

Khurge-Khalbin, Sayan's clan

lama, Buddhist monk

maykhabsha, shaman's headdress

Modon Kharnaga, Volodya's clan

nemerge, White shaman's cape

Neryelge, Thunder Dance

obo, sacred place often marked with a pile of stones on top of a mountain

orgay, shaman's horns

ongons, spirits shamans call down at the *Shanar*

Serge, Hitching Post Tree

Shanar, dedication ceremony for a shaman

tarag, traditional Buryat dairy dish like a milky cheese

Thirteen Northern Spirits, the spirits that live near Lake Baikal and are protectors of shamanism.

Tohorulkha, Bringing up the Dust Ritual

toibur, drumstick

toli, shaman's mirror

udkha, hereditary shaman root spirit

Ur Tree, one of the trees in the birch grove at the *Shanar*

zagalme, red arrowheads inserted into the trunk of an offered birch

zala, red tassels pinned on participants whose souls were "knocked out"

Zalma, Offering Tree

Zarin, shaman with the highest rank who has completed all the *Shanar* rituals. Today there is only one living *Zarin*.

Credits

The majority of the chants, conversations, and statements in this book were recorded during the *Shanar* ritual in August of 2000. Translations from Buryat are by Sayan Zhambalov, Virlana Tkacz, and Wanda Phipps.

The chants include Seseg Balzhinimayeva's Chant to Her Ritual Objects, which is quoted in "The Sacred Grounds" and constitutes all the examples of White shaman chants in "The Ritual Objects." Seseg's White Cleansing Chant is quoted in "The Cleansing" and her Giving Breath to the Tree in "The Offering." Excerpts from Volodya Zhaltsapov's Chant to his Ancestor Spirits are cited in "The Fading Light of a Golden Afternoon." All quotations in "Giving Thanks" are from Seseg's Chant of Thanks to the Four Directions. The chant quoted on page 6 and all the examples of Black shaman chants in "The Ritual Objects" are excerpts from Bayir Rinchinov's Chant to His Ritual Objects which first appeared as "Master of the Drum: A Buryat Shaman's Chant" in the Winter 2000 issue of *Shaman's Drum*, pp. 30–39. Bayir's narrative quotes from the ritual are supplemented by statements from his lecture and conversations at Union Theological Seminary, New York, March 8–9, 1999.

The song "We Play on the Rays of the Sun" on pages 18–19 was originally recorded by Tsyben Zhamtsarano in the summer of 1908 from Dugazhab Batuev in the village of Bada. The translation was first used in the production of Yara's *Flight of the White Bird*, at La MaMa Experimental Theatre in March 1999. It was printed in issue 51 of *Agni Review*, the literary journal published by Boston University. The song "Every Steppe Has Its own Eagle" on page 81 is a traditional *Neryelge* or Thunder Dance that would have been sung by the Children of Heaven during a *Shanar* in the Buryat Aga Region. The translation was first used in *Flight of the White Bird* and also appeared in *Agni Review 51*. The song "Are Those Swans" on pages 125–126 was translated by Sayan Zhambalov, Virlana Tkacz, Wanda Phipps, and Tom Lee. The translation was first used in *Flight of the White Bird*. The song "Till the Sun Sets," page 130 and 179, is also a

Thunder Dance Song. Yara artists recorded the Tumen Zhargalan Folk Ensemble in Aga singing this song in 1997. It is the title track on the CD *Sing Till the Sun Sets: Folk Ensembles from the Aginsk-Buryat Region of Siberia,* which includes Yara's field recordings from this trip (Global Village Music, 2001). Sayan Zhambalov's poem "My Eyes Are the Shimmering Waters" was translated by Sayan Zhambalov, Virlana Tkacz, and Wanda Phipps. It was first performed in *Flight of the White Bird* and published in *Agni* 54.

The swan legend on page 12 is based on the Buryat Chronicles and is the origin myth of the Khori Buryats. It was the topic for *Virtual Souls,* Yara's first collaborative theater piece with the Buryat artists that premiered at La MaMa in January 1997. The shaman legend about the eagle on page 17 was recorded in the nineteenth century by Matvey Khangalov and published in M. N. Khangalov, *Sobraniye sochinenie* [Collected Works] (Ulan Ude: Buryatskoe Knizhniye Izdatelstvo, 1958), volume II, pp. 141–142. The legend about the five animals on page 79 can be found in Khangalov, volume II, pp. 11–12. The link between this story and the animals in the chant was first noted by Dashinima Dugarov.

All photographs are by Alexander Khantaev except the photos of the Mother and Father on page 18, the Children on page 25, and Dulma on page 64, which are by Virlana Tkacz. The portrait of Alexander Khantaev on pages 23 and 191 is by Sayan Zhambalov. The drawings of the *bardag* and the *horbo* are by Sayan Zhambalov. The photo of Virlana Tkacz on page 190 is by V. Voronin. The photo of Wanda Phipps on page 191 is by Joel Schlemowitz. The photo of the Yara Arts Group production on page 191 is by Margaret Morton and the graphic is by Volodymyr Klyuzko.

Suggested Readings

Balzer, Marjorie Mandelstam, editor. *Shamanic World: Ritual and Lore of Siberia and Central Asia.* Armonk, N.Y.: North Castle Books, 1997.

Banzarov, Dorji. "The Black Faith or Shamanism Among the Mongols" (1846). Translated from the Russian by Jan Nattier and John R. Krueger. *Mongolian Studies* (Bloomington) no. 7 (1981–82), pp. 53–91.

Bashkuyev, Gennadi. *The Buryats: Tradition and Culture.* Ulan Ude: Soyol Publishers, 1995.

Dugarov, Dashinima. *Istoricheskiye korni belogo shamanstva na materiale obryadovogo folklora buryat* [The historical roots of White shamanism based on the ritual folklore of the Buryats]. Moscow: Nauka, 1991.

Humphrey, Caroline with Urgunge Onon. *Shamans and Elders: Experience, Knowledge and Power among the Daur Mongols.* Oxford: Clarendon Press, 1996.

Khangalov, M. N. *Sobraniye sochinenie* [Collected Works]. Ulan Ude: Buryatskoe Knizhniye Izdatelstvo, 1958.

"Master of the Drum: A Buryat Shaman's Chant," translated by Sayan Zhambalov, Virlana Tkacz, and Wanda Phipps in *Shaman's Drum*, no. 54 (Winter 2000), pp. 30–39.

Sarangerel. *Riding Windhorses: A Journey into the Heart of Mongolian Shamanism.* Rochester, Vt.: Destiny Books, 2000.

Vitebsky, Piers. *The Shaman.* Boston: Little, Brown and Co., 1995.

The Authors

Sayan Zhambalov, Virlana Tkacz, and Wanda Phipps have been translating Buryat poetry since 1996. Their translations have been performed at the La MaMa Experimental Theatre and the Poetry Project at St. Mark's Church and were published in *Agni Review, Terra Nova, Two Lines*, and *Shaman's Drum*. They have received three New York State Council on the Arts Translation Grants, as well as the Witter Bynner Foundation for Poetry Translation Award for their work.

Virlana Tkacz directs the Yara Arts Group, a resident company at La MaMa Experimental Theatre in New York. She has made twenty-seven original theater pieces with Yara by bringing together fragments of plays, poetry, song, and chant. Since 1996 she has worked with Buryat artists to create six original theater pieces. Virlana's work with Wanda Phipps on translations has also been awarded the National Theater Translation Prize and the *Agni Review* Poetry Translation Prize and the National Endowment for the Arts Poetry Translation Fellowship. She is a recipient of three Fulbright Fellowships.

Sayan Zhambalov, writer, actor, and singer, comes from a family of Buryat poets, blacksmiths, and shamans. Considered one of the best Buryat artists of his generation, he has been recognized with the title Honored Artist of the Russian Federation. He and Erzhena Zhambalov are a popular duo in Buryatia, and he heads Uragsha, a traditional music ensemble that has performed at the World Music Institute in New York. A book of his poems was published in Ulan Ude. He has worked with Yara, collecting Buryat folk songs, legends, and shaman chants and creating original theater pieces.

Wanda Phipps is a poet, performer, and translator. She is the author of six books of poetry including the most recent *Field of Wanting: Poems of Desire* (Blaze Vox Books). Her poems have appeared in more than one hundred literary journals, anthologies, and CD compilations. She has been a contributing editor for numerous literary journals and has coordinated several poetry reading series in New York. She is a founding member of Yara and a recipient of a New York Foundation for the Arts Poetry Fellowship.

Alexander Khantaev's photographs have appeared in numerous publications in Buryatia and he has exhibited with the Union of Photographers of Buryatia. In the summer of 1999, he first traveled with Yara to the Ust-Orda Buryat Region and photographed the sacred island of Olkhon on Lake Baikal. Photographs that appear in this book were in his exhibit "Portraits of Siberian Shamans" at the Open Space Gallery in Saratoga Springs and at La MaMa Galleria in New York. His exhibitions, "Meetings in Mongolia" and "Koliada" were based on photographs he took during Yara's research expeditions.

Yara Arts Group creates original theater pieces that explore the cultures of the East and attain universality in the telling. For more than twenty-five years their shows have been performed at La MaMa Experimental Theatre in New York, where Yara is a resident company, and abroad in Ulan Ude, Kyiv, Lviv, Kharkiv, Bishkek, and Ulan Baatar. Yara also produces poetry readings, concerts, art exhibits, and workshops. For more information write Yara Arts Group, 306 E 11th St. #3B, New York, NY 10003 or visit our website http://www.brama.com/yara.

Books of Related Interest

The Gift of Shamanism
Visionary Power, Ayahuasca Dreams, and Journeys to Other Realms
by Itzhak Beery
Foreword by John Perkins

Shamanic Transformations
True Stories of the Moment of Awakening
Edited by Itzhak Beery

Shapeshifting
Techniques for Global and Personal Transformation
by John Perkins

Speaking with Nature
Awakening to the Deep Wisdom of the Earth
by Sandra Ingerman and Llyn Roberts

Sacred Plant Medicine
The Wisdom in Native American Herbalism
by Stephen Harrod Buhner
Foreword by Brooke Medicine Eagle

Plant Spirit Shamanism
Traditional Techniques for Healing the Soul
by Ross Heaven and Howard G. Charing
Foreword by Pablo Amaringo

Original Wisdom
Stories of an Ancient Way of Knowing
by Robert Wolff

Ayahuasca Medicine
The Shamanic World of Amazonian Sacred Plant Healing
by Alan Shoemaker

INNER TRADITIONS • BEAR & COMPANY
P.O. Box 388
Rochester, VT 05767
1-800-246-8648
www.InnerTraditions.com

Or contact your local bookseller